The Gang Capitol

The Gang Capitol

The Art of Gang War and Racism Behind It

Raymoutez Price

Library of Congress Control Number:		2013908017
ISBN:	Hardcover	978-1-4836-3546-0
	Softcover	978-1-4836-3545-3
	Ebook	978-1-4836-3547-7

Rev. date: 05/31/2013

To order additional copies of this book, contact:
Xlibris Corporation
1-888-795-4274
www.Xlibris.com
Orders@Xlibris.com
132636

The war bug, a tribal ancestry, black men and black-on-black crimes, the new era of the Zulu warfare, the gang life, the rise of the infamous Bloods and Crips gangs, from the East Coast to the West Coast, born and made in America

THE TAKEOVER

This vintage book is thoroughly reviewed and studied by a known and actual bonafide ex-affiliate member of the notorious Watts Compton Avenue Crips 95.7um Str. Some statements and names may be changed and deliberately fabricated to protect the innocent. My true purpose is to allow you to understand how gangs and their systems operate. So I put you in the heart of the battlefield. I will enlighten you with stats and facts. The affiliation factors demonstrate how some cities and states are overrun and held hostage, how some gangs mimic the essence of leeches or vampires as they attach to environments and clamp down, viciously sucking the blood marrow, draining its prey dry, devouring anything that gets in its way. This overpowering war machine shows no sign of depleting itself, but it continues to multiply fast, spreading throughout various parts of the country.

After reading this book, your mind will be placed directly in the center of the battlefield. My views are certified and genuine facts. I have met many affiliates from Los Angeles, Chicago, Alabama, and Indiana. During my journey throughout many different diverse cities and states, I noticed that every place endures most of the same "pities." The facts are the same shit, just from a different toilet! Nothing has changed but accents and styles and time zones; however, it's all the same black-on-black lynching. We all play the same game. Some players in the game are more serious in certain areas and some in diverse places. The violence is very dormant. Every city has its own peculiar differences and its Achilles' heel—the dark forbidden places that most people rather fly past in a helicopter or speed by in the fastest vehicle known to mankind, rather than walk through on a dark, misty night, creeping through a dark alley confronted by the elements of the hood, so menacing and terrifying that the grim reaper got caught in the wrong place, at the wrong time. He was jacked and robbed, chased out naked, just a black cloud of smoke followed his presence. You must have a ghetto privilege, hood pass, to enter. If you look like you don't belong to this environment, you're subject to be assaulted.

Notoriously known as Killerfornia (a.k.a. Killer Cali), the City of Angels and Demons, the gang activities are catastrophic, more deadly than AIDS and cancer combined. The gangs spread like viruses; any city it attaches itself to becomes consumed liked wildfire. While the entire city is held hostage, every corner, every street, every house, every stone and even the sand in the children playgrounds becomes stained with the untainted blood of the innocent. The infamous Crips and Bloods can be located in many states and countries, which the cultures have adapted to many new forms, politically. In some states, it has become a fad. The only difference is its structure and gang political point of views, but in California, the gangs have been demoralized and defaced, compared in the same category as terrorist such as Taliban crazed maniacs who blow planes to smithereens and crash them into buildings! Affiliated with high-profile, high-caliber gangs that add to the simplicities of increased homicides committing along with offensive crimes across the board, causing a Desert Storm in America!

California has implications that apply to all severe and the most critical chaotic gang members located in areas where the highest crime rates occur. These new and effectively innovative gang injunctions are clamping down on the most violent individuals that are involved in the most heinous crimes. The gang injunction can increase a gang member's jail sentences with an additional twenty-five years, ran concurrent with existing charges. If that doesn't work, gang enhancements and gang indictments surely will get the job done! Easier said than done, eradicating the streets by issuing out dinosaur years, depleting the criminal elements, one by one, until it's more like May-berry. If you use profanity, you can be arrested and sentenced to prison. In other words, cursing would simply be a high offensive crime. It seems imaginary, the days that lie ahead far in the future when murder and all crimes shall be a thing of the past! Cutting-edge technology, science, and the reprimanding of the laws are redundant and inevitable. Divine demise becomes every criminal's futuristic journey!

These things are very familiar to me because I'm a certified Five Bar member. (Bars mean I have stripes as if I were a coronel or sergeant in the armed forces.) Stripes are achieved by the amounts of high-caliber gang-related work you put in. Unlike the subliminal movies such as *Colors* and *Boyz n the Hood*, it gave Crips and Bloods an abstracted visual impression that labeled every movie thereafter in Hollywood, barely touching the true surface that everyone was so afraid of painting a more factual horrific and vivid picture of what truly transpired, not evading the true factors working behind the scenes. Crimes throughout California are portrayed through the Hollywood lens, purposely designed and precisely orchestrated to seem dismissive and dormant. Those movies were more like comedy, a laughingstock, as if the film director was forbidden and handcuffed, not allowed to illustrate the true blood, guts and gore in the streets, uncut and pure raw vintage action from front cover to the back cover! After all, it was 1984. Special effects were not that effective! The movies *Colors* and *Boyz n the Hood* were based on real reviews and actual events. Its views were sugarcoated, not fully detailing the true stories that were unseen and untold! The real magnitude of war effects and the "rules of engagement" are detrimental.

Gang wars can sometimes consist of many gang-related shootings. Sometimes one gang can indulge in as many as six or eight shootings throughout the entire

City of Angels, attempting to find the responsible group who initiated the shootings against them, which creates a floodgate of shootings. Usually, when someone is shot or killed in Los Angeles, it is better for the gang to know exactly who initiated the gang shooting. Otherwise, if the gang victimized in the shooting has no clue at all who the attackers were, expect calculated repercussion, activating a deadly nuclear in cognitive, Negroes' self-annihilation button that kills two for the price of one! All out! All in! Turned up hoods will go out head hunting, seeking to destroy all their rival enemies, not knowing who did it. They just say, "Get them all!" Quadrants mount up, and crews are dispatched, directed toward all suspected archenemies. One neighborhood can cause so much damage in one day, resulting in numerous assaulted victims and numerous individuals gunned down, causing a domino effect. Los Angeles gangs play by this rule of return fire, the revenge tick for tack game. You hit one hood in the city in gun play that one hood can cause all the other hoods to jump in headfirst, pistols blazing, shooting first, asking questions later. And each hood has this mentality. If we don't know who the rival enemy was involved in the shooting, the exact, precise hood that was involved, then we attack everything moving. We just hit them all. And some hoods, for example, the Hoover Crips, simply at war with the entire City of Angels. Their enemy list is larger than the list of fallen soldiers they have lost due to a full-fledged gang war. Some Crips hoods can beef with up to over twelve different Crips hoods at one time, not even including the X-factor. The Bloods usually come in like a cleanup crew, getting any one left behind sporting the color blue, asking nothing, just shooting. The domino effect that occurs in certain hot zones which gang activities are extremely intense, shootings are a normal occurrences. The cops couldn't report so many random shootings which occurs all at one time. After all the entire city was engaged in all out warfare. Lack of police presence non existent on certain blocks whom have been hit in a barrage of all out gang attempted shootings sometimes neighborhoods are hit four or five times in one day, this being a hobby and daily activity for most gang affiliates. Not one block was safe while war was in effect because enemies hunt for statistics. Sometimes they play unruly. If you hit innocent bystanders on their turf, they return the favor of casualties in your turf, "tick for tack". Like playing freeze tag your it in this game. Big difference with the game of life one shot one tag and the game could simply cause you your life. When war is effective, traps are set. The wind whistles like the old cowboy movies. The silence is vital. The people hide inside, refusing to walk around. No one hangs out when Los Angeles is at war.

We know our city. We know the rules. We are the ones who have survived. We know that during real wars, you can't find a soul anywhere. The dogs and cats don't even run through the yards. They go inside their cat litter boxes, and the dogs hide inside their dog houses. The birds fly south when a storm is coming, Well, since they are already south, they fly back north when the shootings start, except the crows and buzzards; they hang around to collect the dead corpses and feast. There are lots of gunfire-injured victims block to block, a natural activity that occurs repeatedly. The City Of Angeles transforms into a futile hunting ground, Sometimes, to a foreigner visiting, the city seems so peaceful to the necked eye. You are unaware of the elusiveness of the detrimental violence. Then everything around you explodes into a spontaneous combustion. The true City of Demons is at work, wreaking havoc. The City of Angels reveals its two different sides: the one side that is violent and the other side that is menacing, ferocious, mind-boggling, and violent. Almost, so to speak. Either way you look at it, its war if you do! It's war if you don't! Gang affiliates walk up, ride up on bikes, jump outs of the cars, and walk by with crews. Some have even dressed up like women and bums, pushing baskets.

This is the art of war in a city that is known for its high murder rate, getting creative with killing, becoming a hobby, a past time. This is the breed. This is how we are raised. Like the movie black hawk down, we are prone to engage in war, like a baby that knows where the mother's breast and its purpose. Instinct guides the child to feed from the mother's breast. We are bred in our environment and we become products of its violence some of us attain to becoming bigger then life street legends with legacies told with violence blood and gore indenting and putting the stamp of approval as one of the elite Ghetto stars sealed and certified to go down as one of the most infamous gangsters of our own history. The most engaged affiliates attain to becoming the most elite ghetto warriors. Because war is so imminent in the city, we learn methods to counterattack. It becomes very complicated to catch an enemy slipping in the city. It has been inflicted so much do to gun-blazing galore that everyone in the entire city becomes trained on what to do and on what not to do in guerrilla warfare. Even old women can instruct you how to survive! Five-year-old kids can give you a good survival lesson, the most recent beef to exist in this decade, which means some hoods pick up new beefs like picking up a high-profiled Playboy bunny call girl / prostitute; example of metamorphosis. Hoods create street conflicts resulting in new enemies added to a prolong list. Like a heavyweight bout, the streets listen, and they talk back. You want to know anything, put your ear to the ground. The streets have its justice creating so many foes. The streets can't hide you. Sooner or later everyone has a number, and when the debt collector arrives to collect, you surely can't hide from what you can't see. All debts paid and cleared, and the streets have slain and claimed another who forgot the rules that apply the deal the streets always offer. Blood in, blood out. The way you live, the way you pay. The way you come in is the way you go out. Every man or boy shall receive it how they have issued it. There is no exception, no crying to momma. Little Boys, a deal is a deal kept, and a deadly date called doom awaits your arrival for I'm the unseen. The place I'm from, I keep it well lit with gasoline, so don't light a match when you arrive because once you lit it, it will remain lit for a very long time. Catch my drift.

Other professionally seasoned warring hoods listen like middle-weight or feather-weight boxing competitors. This scale of war travels when two big gangs even in number and participates in a well-matched, almost-identical brute force applied, known for smashing a term used to describe destroying or annihilating the enemy, the creative skills used, count how many victims were shot, how many casualties of death inflicted, in the shortest amount of time. The streets watch, look, and listen, giving the famous word of mouth and hood announcement precisely and accurately: who's doing what, who's up, and who's actually winning the engaged warfare. The channel 7 eyewitness news; records are kept. The ghetto has its own reports which results many unknown factors which are too hot for television too raw to even mention but oh the streets gossip always knowing the tinniest slightest small detail someone had forgotten to mention which always highlight the true facts behind the scene. The newest feud explicitly defines the old way that war infected the entire city. This type of warfare wasn't just the way two gangs had done it. This was the way the entire state of California enforced its street laws. Los Angeles just happened to be the center of the hub, the gang capitol. All-out warfare was the game we played. Scratch the Play Station and X-box. We played the real 3D high-definition. Catch you off guard, and that was your ass. The war between the (Watts Baby Loc Crips 103rd, Grape Street Watts Crips) versus the (IEast Coast Crips 97th, 89th, Q102nd, 76th) was one of the most gruesome wars of the decade, which happened in the year 2006. During this decade the beef between the two mega gangs was nearly as gruesome as the wars of the (1980s and 1990s), which involved the following beefs: (ES East Coast 62nd, 66th, 68th, 69th Streets) versus (52nd Broadway Gangster Crips); (79th, 77th, 84th, 89th ES Mad Family Swan Bloods) versus (ES East Coast Crips 62nd, 66th, 68th, 69th, 89th, 97th, 76th); (WS83GC Eight Tray Gangster Crips) versus (Rolling Sixties Crips). Mega heavyweight wars: (WS Hoover Crips Gang 52th, 74th, 83rd, 92nd, 94th,107th,112nd) versus (Rolling Sixties ('60s), Rolling Forties ('40s), Rolling Nineties ('90s), Rolling Hundreds (100s) along with all neighborhood Crips gangs, uniting to battle all Hoover Crips and the infamous 83 Gangster Crips and their allies such as School Yard Crips (SYC), Shotgun Crips (SGC), Kitchen Crips (KCG), Pay-Back Crips (PBC), Broadway Gangster Crips (BGC), Back Street Crips (BSC), Four Tray Gangster Crips (FTGC), Avalon Gangster Crips (AGC), Du-Rock Crips (DRC), Nine, Nine Mafia Crips (99MC), Playboy Style Crips (PBSC), Playboy Hustler Crips (PBHC), MFGC Mansfield Gangster Crips, Gear Gang Crips (GGC), Imperial Village Crips (IVC). Unfortunately, some of their allies ended up on the Hoover's enemies list. They obtained so many enemies that the newer generation renamed themselves Hoover Criminals, replacing the Crips with Criminal. This didn't sit well with the original members of the Hoover set, but with guards and dictatorship changing hands so randomly, no one had control of their set. So they became renegades of the city, the first gang to write "Bk Ck Ok" on the walls; but in the future, this would come back to haunt them because they once were the biggest, most fearsome, deepest gangs in prison.

Every decade, the tides changed. Being young, the youth don't think ten years ahead. They only think on a day-to-day basis. Dishonoring the Crips, many gangs tend to let the Hoover, fight their own battles, not getting involved to assist them since they denounced the Crips' anonymity; and that's when the infamous Hoover began to become the pigeon or sitting ducks on the streets and in prison, catching hell from all angles. They received more casualties on their side, and countless lives were blown away like a blistering wind than ever before. They refuse acknowledge how much their allies had done while assisting them, taking some of the applied pressure off them by engaging other Crips sets who were not even their rival enemies, for the purpose to prove loyalty and their own camaraderie, to prove that they were down to ride and put in work. They Hoovers had failed at applying structure and order, which was depleted with the change of guard and the new dying breed of soldiers who always curse themselves, announcing how they had no regards for living or killing,. life expectancy only 25 years which usually became the magic number that many affiliated gangsters met their demise, always speaking to existent their own deaths sounded so macho like as if it was destiny until that time had come. "I have never seen a man cry until I have seen a man die." When death is close, men run and hide, fearing the worse, fearing the debt collector; but among mortal men, they are so macho, so talkative, so hood. But once that last breath becomes so hard to gasp for, it becomes a battle to breathe that last taste of air. Only men who have come this close understand how deep this terminology is. The pain is intense, and unlike anything earth has to offer during the brief eternity, you can feel your hell and you plead to God to save you, pledging to change if you could only get one more shot at it to go back and warn the many fallen Crips and Bloods and gangs all across the world that hell is real; and it's what you make it. The pain is unimaginable, unthinkable. The gates open, releasing you from death's clutches; and you are able to breathe. You know the gang life has a deeper cost to pay, so you try to figure how you can warn the masses with skills you have been ordained with, a gift of talking. Maybe it's in writing, so you begin telling the story of the lifestyle of gang war and activities. Some youth may misunderstand your purpose and try to motivate themselves to misconceive the message, attempting to be the monster in the streets, or of the story told, overlooking all the facts that come after the glory of me putting aspects together to paint the picture. To gain the attention of the masses, it was orchestrated for me to pull the youth in with the same blood and gore they like hearing and listening to because this is how they listen and communicate, so I have used my mind to capture your thought and plant the truth. Understand that the story is not meant to train you to become ruthless killers, but if you can't change, add some order to your lives because I have lived the lifestyle, and I have told my story. Now you know some truths. Use it to change because a true debt collector awaits you. Your home boy that was a merciless street legend ain't so tough anymore after meeting the real debt collector. In death, a man cries for life. He begs for God to let him live.

Read the facts, listen to the story, but don't become consumed by the violence. If I get too gruesome, realign yourself and turn it down. Understand that there is a moral and just purpose involved to awaken the sleep walkers shackled in mind.

The Hoover Crips were identical in comparison with the city called Watts. They bragged about being scandalous, trifling, not able to be trusted, and willing to turn on you in seconds, no matter who you were. No one wanted to move in their hood because when you walk to the store, you might not make it back home. In their hood, you were a prime target. Back in the days, the Hoovers in Prison were the biggest, baddest powerhouse moving; but time changed, and other Crips gangs united, replacing them as power structures. Such as the Hub and Wub, Compton and Watts, even the Neighborhood and Rolling cards united with staggering numbers. The Hoovers Criminals disassociated with Crips because of the almighty big ego that we are the biggest and the baddest. Sometimes too much pride can be a commodity! As times changed in decades, the Hoovers were found not to be so invincible as the other gangs. Their enemies, who were fellow Crips gangs, began picking them off. No one wanted to be a Hoover. It was way too dangerous with them warring inwardly and with their beefs with the Hispanic South X Los (SxL13). They nearly became extinct as many of their enemies focused on their neighborhood word traveled fast like a wounded lion in a brawl the many predators noticed how vulnerable the 112 Hoovers were and begin feasting nearly wiping an entire click of the Hoovers out of existence. The 112 Hoovers were considered by most in the gang world as the most less active Hoover set in existence because of full engagement with two other powerhouses: The Denver Lane Bloods (DLB), pure head hunters, surrounded by Rolling 100's UGC-BLCG-BCG along with beefing with the SxL, a very dangerous Cholo Hispanic gang that became racist—not only were they killing Hoover Crips because they couldn't tell the difference they considered all blacks to be Hoovers, they just began killing blacks at random rates, period, and writing "murder all niggers" on the wall. That's when engagement in wars became more complicated, especially after one year when the SxL were killing innocent blacks at will. The two crimes that put a stamp on their war tactics happened once they had killed a twelve-year-old little girl. That same year, they killed an elderly black man and stuffed his body inside a trash can. He was undiscovered and missing for some days. During the early 1990s, the Mexican gangs called a peace treaty after the famous Bloods and Crips peace treaty of 1992, which only lasted for two years. In some places, it was never peace at all! The Mexican gangs called a ceasefire, and the wars were over with the snap of fingers. Overnight, the murder rate declined to nearly 40 percent over the next few months during the peace treaty of all hispanics. If a Hispanic was involved in shooting one of their own kind, they were dealt with accordingly to their structure. There was order after a while, with the prison riots igniting the hate spilled out toward the streets. And now a new breed of war begins to blossom. People begin to walk around with a heavy tension in

the air, upset that rules were set in motion that they were not able to talk with
blacks whom they had grown up with. Some of them were their best friends, but
because of the racial tensions in the air, families begin to become targets. When
gangs couldn't reach out and touch the members, the gangs resorted to killing
family members. Children, old men, and women became targets and the blacks
didn't play by these rules. They usually shot children and old women and old men
by accident, shooting at rivals but this new war had no rules, and some gangs grew
so angry it became brutal, a tick for a tack. This becomes an orchestrated plot
designed to deplete the black race, knowing that war ends lives. If you kill a black
family, you know that gang will do the same to your family. Now you have tempers
flaring because of those who think that you can kill someone and the boomerang
effect doesn't comply too you. After all they are known for killing just like you
are! So deception is involved, and someone has thought out some genius plan
of demise to decimate the people because gang violence go as far back as racism
being the anchor. Nowadays, so many beefs exist with Hispanic and black gangs.
It's almost an all-out race war in the City of Angels.

The Rolling 100's card consists of Under Ground Crips (UGC), Neighborhood
Crips (111th NHC), Block Crips (BCG), and Raymond Avenue Crips (RAC).
For all these sets, war was in full stealth smash mode despite the infamous racist
murders. The Crips and Bloods continued to inflict casualties upon the Hoovers,
and all other black gangs were involved in an all-out complete war against each
other—black-on-black crime. No structure is applied; there's no order. They all
were engaged like ticking time bombs, and their hate was directed for only the
blacks. They hated each other more than the Klan hated them. The only time
blacks seem to unite as one group, Crips and Bloods, only happened once we
all were headed to the penitentiary, where racist wars were so imminent; and the
Crips and Bloods' worse vital enemies were the Southern Mexican. But the Crips
and Bloods were allies with the Northern Mexicans, who also couldn't stand the
sight of Southern Mexicans; and their beefs were all-out fueled, and they killed
each other on site. Regardless of the Northern Mexicans' red flag color, they
were the best allies the Crips and Bloods had in prison, the best-kept secret. The
Northern Mexicans spoke better English and had less racist agendas. They seem
to have lived around blacks so long they had picked up our slang, walk, talk, and
attitudes. The only help the112 Hoovers had were the 107 Hoovers, but they had
their own problems, the same exact enemies the 112 Hoovers had acquired. The
107 Hoovers could only do so much to help the almost depleted 112 Hoovers.
After losing so many soldiers, they begin to lose grip of their claimed turf. Enemies
got word that their front lines were weak, and they had come out to feast, attacking
them like a wild bunch of piranhas. Their greatest weapon was evasiveness, staying
out of sight or inside the house, Sometimes even moving out of the city became a
very viable antic of survival, doing their dirt, and going home, which was very far
away. Some 112 Hoover just simply changed sets, switching over to the other more

effective, more gruesome, war-prone Hoover sets, for example. The original 74th, 52nd, and the up and rising notorious 83rd Hoovers were just as deadly as the first and original infamous 74th. Hoover Crips, huge in numbers, all cold, calculated killers. Being from the Hoover gang in the 1980s up to early 1990s meant killing your enemies and having a screw-the-world attitude. These dudes went to war with so many mega-powerhouse gangs at one time. They were all known shooters, and the casualties of war rate upon their enemies were extremely high. They set the standards of all-out war, well respected by few and hated by many hoods, emulated or feared, engaging in war with them, because they kept the peddle along with the meddle, smashing at will. But of course, the tables always take a turn when the opposing sides receive the first round draft pick, the newest ball player! Changing the game, setting new standards and rules, all of a sudden, the enemies became the foe and began smashing different up-and-coming players involved in this new era. New-decade war tactics increase many deceased Conrad's on both sides of the fence. So much Blood spilled between the two different Crips sets over nearly two decades. Hundreds were murdered. Peace between the two seems nonexistent. The older, original crews of gladiators either were dead or in prison for life. Or some freed their minds from the shackles, breaking free, becoming smarter and matured, putting behind them the gang life, enduring a newfound life. Some, finding faith and belief and God and true purpose, moved far away. Some chose to continue to live around to help defuse the burning fire that they had caused to become intensely ignited and out of control. They figured the least they could do, after all the years of involvement as Crips. Now it was time to help somehow decrease the violence or counsel the stemming fires.

Throughout all the years, adding wood to the intense inferno in the ghetto, it was time to add water to put the fire out for good. It's time to wake the sleeping giants. Every decade, the players change and so does the rules and environments. People are trying to change what they have started, which is harder than you can imagine. People follow more wrong attributes of failure and criminal acts, compared with following someone of purpose and good direction. Those of you who were not familiar with the lingo, slang, or neighborhood settings of *Colors* or *Boyz n the Hood* couldn't identify who was a Crips or Blood. Those movies were evasive to the true identities of the Crips or Bloods. Do you want to be able to visualize the true personalities of the Crips and Bloods? Read the books by Monster Kody and Stanley (Tookie) Williams (RIP), Big Tookie, author of many children's books *Blue Rage, Black Redemption.*" These are great books Tookie Williams nominee of the Noble Peace Prize while on death row, waiting for execution. Monster Kody is the author of *Monster,* a story depicting the true realities of gangs in Los Angeles. Both books will horrify and intrigue you at the same time. That is if you would like to hear the raw uncut truth. Truth being told, the gang atmosphere is more sophisticated than any Harvard student can identify or study. You can create a census as regards studying the gang population and culture, and your facts will not be accurate. To know the beast, you must live in the belly of the beast. The reason Stanley (Tookie) Williams and Monster Kody's books sold many copies is because they were products of their environment they wrote about. They lived inside the belly of the beast that gave them street creditability. Being young, black, and affiliated with the two powerhouses, the Crips and Bloods, to being a part of the environment and a soldier at war, you were familiar with the lingo when they spoke of put in work. By all means necessary, you knew it meant going out hunting like Zulu warriors (tribe against tribe) by means of strategic tactics: sabotage = setups. It is just straight-up ugly, down and dirty, grimy, gritty, filthy cutthroat guerrilla warfare. We have no leaders. Once you have been proven in the art of war, your portfolio speaks for itself. During times of conflict, the thrill of stepping up, side by side with your comrades, is pleasure. You become linked as one! A unit, a family bond grows consolidated. As each warrior indulges himself in war, he gains significant amounts of respect by inflicting great amounts of damage to the enemy based on his performance and fatalities delivered. He begins to advance to the next level, gaining stripes based on the one who has the most successful amount of missions and who has the last say if we go or stay. We do our research just like the army infantry. We rely on molds, traitors to their own, spies! Don't be mesmerized that sometimes we get details of ambush from the regular Jane or Joe, a neutral = non affiliate, neither Blood nor Crips. Neutral people are sometimes senior citizens who have been oppressed by the neighborhood gang's choke hold and brutality. They even become a product of their own environment to the point that some of the most violent, disrespectful members of the gangs insult and target them in senseless crimes. When the gang members are murdered or seriously hurt, the senior citizens actually celebrate as if a shackle had been loosened, allowing them flexibility to maneuver freely throughout a neighborhood in which they are the deed holders of their own property, but they are hostages to their environment. They become exhilarated and astounded that some other courageous gang members on the other side of the tracks had balls enough to do what they could dream of doing after suffering brute force and the humility of not being respected on their own land, while scum come in and out, to and from, daily spitting and urinating on the land that is entitled to them, rightfully belonging to them. They become targets of retributions, being shot and gunned down for nearly standing up, demanding peace and quiet, instructing the local hoodlums to steer away from their fence or yard. They are threatened, sometimes even beaten to a bloody pulp, in a handicapped mismatch! A senior resident can look at the up and coming members and predict, having a premonition of the ones who would die next. They were often right, staring into their dark, deep, pitch-black eyes, seeing nothing but a deep abyss, a hole that was empty, without life or concern or pity for anyone. His deeds are reckoned with his doom for he had no mercy and repentance, and redemption was to him a weakness! Being an elder living and watching people die around you for nearly sixty-five years, they could feel and the knew that death was in the making and followed the wicked street dwellers like a shadow. They knew when a man was so evil and his end was close and what lies below! Lots of innocent by standers were affected by warfare. Children, babies, and seniors were all victims and some have even been murdered when stray bullets were misfired because of a rookie's mistake. The most lethal warrior fights a war and wins without even firing one shot. He can get down and dirty with the most elite, but he rather diffuses a situation beforehand, knowing how much damage he can inflict. He knows that trouble is so easy to find but so hard to get yourself out of. So it doesn't pay to go around looking for trouble. You just might find exactly what you're not looking for. For a veteran, knows the methods applied, along with the rank of an individual, are based on the casualties of their missions and the amount of violence used. When you have become a five-star war vet, your five senses have become honed and acute. You're able to profile the difference of a rookie compared with a professional and seasoned veteran. Most uneducated rookies always die fast and young because they fail to do their research in the art of war, or they simply have poor instructors who send them out on a limb with no advice. Generals and lieutenants are familiar with the conduct and basic rules of war, the doe's and dont's. That is how he has survived this concrete guerrilla warfare for so many years. Rookies normally commit fatal mistakes that cause them their lives or their comrades' lives. Gangs have infantries. Sad to say, most enormous hoods don't have great structure, which means some generals and lieutenants from these over sized gangs don't give out great detail or instructions to their soldiers, so they become sacrificed like pawns in a chess game. Smaller gangs are a different breed of soldier. Because of their small numbers, the word of "we are at war" travels fast, and we begin to mount all of our soldiers to prevent casualties on our side and inflict major damage to the other side. You can't hit what you can't see. Evasiveness, along with swift, sturdy precision, proves to be highly catastrophic and fatal. Big gangs lack the ability to communicate and reach very few of their soldiers in time of conflict, therefore leaving their soldiers out to dry, like walking zombies or cattle marching vaguely into the slaughter house. The bigger the hoods, the bigger the caps, and the bigger the peelings. Small gangs who beef with big gangs are often underdogs. But they are most dangerous with every strike. As the streets talk, they expect the small gangs to be annihilated in a matter of days. Little did they know the power the small chew-chew possessed, the heart and the will, not to retreat nor surrender. Proved to be larger gangs' vulnerable weakness is always the pride factor. They gather in large numbers, celebrating victory before battle, laughing and joking about how small we are, only three members strong, and how they were going to invade our turf and take over it. Larger gangs always like to boast their numbers by hanging out on the fronts in times of war, a very critical large mistake. Thanks to a few spies and moles in their hood, who are always reliable as the neighborhood hood rat, term for females whom degrade themselves, we locate their positions and send out a scout. When he gives us the green light, we mount up the Calvary, a bunch of medieval pipe hitting, bone crushing brothers, ready to bring pain, equipped with an enormous amount of artillery, three or four carloads of the best soldiers. We lie low and wait for the perfect moment to strike like a black mamba. As we locate a blind spot, we use the element of surprise, inflicting large amounts of injuries and fatalities swiftly and bluntly, giving them nowhere to run, nowhere to hide. Screams and cries and grunts of dismay hurl along with those discharged .223's David has slain Goliath! Living in a jungle, you must transform yourself into a monster if you don't want to fall as prey. That means shaking hands with the devil. This means be ready to kill. That's the only way you can bring down Goliath. Many men say they don't hate, but I know hate breeds envy, and the only way to destroy the enemy is to destroy the existence of his character to dehumanize him in the same breath as spit on the concrete. The mind-set of an active gang affiliate is always to conquer and destroy. His environment has taught nothing less than eat or be eaten, the same survival tactics that apply in the animal kingdom. The media mostly always blame all-out warfare on drugs, but the truth is there always other scenarios prove why wars take form, simple boneheaded reasons such as two dudes screwing the same female, or two guys from different gangs who simply don't like each other from the gate. One murders the other, creating a domino effect; but rules do apply because if the murdered victim is a non rank or nobody, don't expect any casualties retribution because no one is going to attempt to pick up one old rusty hammer. On the other hand, if the murdered victim was a certified factor to his hood, a reputable ranked fallen soldier, add a new enemy to the list because retaliation is a must; and if your hood ranks out, it means non retaliation. Remember, this is the law of the jungle. If any animal is wounded during an attack, it is considered weak. So at your weakest point, lions lie in the den, waiting for the moment to strike and kill. The word of mouth travels very fast, which opens up the floodgates to additional enemies you're at war with. Some hoods, especially behemoths hoods, sometimes endure battles, fending off eight beefs simultaneously at one time, while an onslaught of attacks occurs from all angles and sides and even fronts. Different hoods simultaneously engage in this military-style guerrilla warfare. Two different (sets) gangs can be out hunting. That tribal taboo Zulu warrior instinct takes over periodically. Two distinctive different (tribes) gangs are out on the prowl, hunting for a common enemy, simultaneously unaware that they are both hunting for an enemy that they both share as a common foe. Upon going out in tribal warfare gang code (missions), two separate tribes engage in conflict while attempting to take down a common enemy. During the brief exchange of hellfire, the prime tribal target lies low, unaware of the missions to cause inflicted casualties directed toward their (tribe) gang. Subsequently, during the hell of rapid gunfire, casualties were imminent on both sides, not knowing both (tribes) gangs, so-called innocent by-standers.

During the hunt, the two (tribes) are out hunting for a common enemy without any knowledge of each other's presence. Fallen soldiers on both sides were the mere results of how catastrophic warfare can occur in Los Angeles, and enemies normally can exist from any disgruntled sort of situation gone bad, resulting in an all-out guerrilla warfare. This means the hood that was being attacked receives credit for the casualties that two enemies from two different (tribes) lost soldiers on their turf. The kicker is later on down the line. The two hoods who were out hunting find out the hidden blind truth of the casualties. They become futile new archenemies, or either they were already fueled hostile enemies. So now their beef reignites if they had some sort of prior disagreement before the hunt resulted in casualties; in the city of Los Angeles, disagreement gets you dead, or it ignites the flames of fury if the two hunting (tribes) gangs were initially allies. Now you have the chain effect. The worldwide Californian recipe of this war is like a syndrome flowing through the entire city of Angels. The most active increased highlighted homicidal, most treacherous, gruesome grueling individuals. Take nothing from anyone, non-tolerant, stand alone, no hostages, no prisoners, the Kamikaze mind-set: "Grab the bulls by the horns." Head-on, straightforward, stand-up approach: "Years of high-end increased war-zoned, war-prone battles transforms normal people into erratic emotionless killing machines." Study each word and paraphrase carefully to depict the mental aspects of depression, oppression, tyranny, physiological warfare, indirectly suppressed four hundred years of distorted, branded, and reprogrammed. Hate of self in modern-day slavery in your own minds, shackled looking in the mirror, killing oneself, the inferior side is the nigger who's afraid, timid, the yes man that which marks a man as he even resents his skin color and the people whom are the same ethnicities which he is in conflict with oneself in the same order as a morphadike confused of his/her gender. Gangs kill each other because of this same sort of confusion and self hate of ones color of skin feeling inferior they kill each other time and time again. Being on top of the world in the killing fields, ranked number 1 in murder rates, nearly tripling the homicidal rates compared with Green Bay, Wisconsin, or some small hick town nearly eighteen years in a row, sad to say, more men, women, and children have died here in America during the renegade black-on-black extermination of the Negroid race. We intend to deplete ourselves out of existence if you put both World Wars 1 and 11 together. Adding the casualties of war, of Afro-Americans you can consider the facts that more Blacks die here on our own turfs. Cities are considered a disaster zone of mass murder and chaos and a self destructing nuclear weapon of massive deadly intentions void of the neutrons and protons needed to create a nuclear explosion. Boom! All the while, the chemical imbalance becomes unstable within the Negroid minds, shackled and stamped, indented, engraved, teaching black men to hate self and anyone who look like him, lab rats in our adopted States, our America, after nearly four hundred years of warfare; yet the state remains unstable within those eighteen years in a row, leading the country with unjust crimes against black men, women, and Children, racking up over seven hundred murders per year, from the years 1979 until 2012.

In this all-out warfare, the black race was nearly depleted and close to becoming extinct in one city alone. This is only the murder rate per Los Angeles only, not including Oakland, San Francisco, Modesto, Richmond, Sacramento, Vallejo, San Diego, San Jose, and the Bay Area. California, the state combined, received its nickname as Killer Cali simply by the grueling murderous numbers alone in forty-five consecutive years, with staggering number of over one thousand homicides committed per year and for eighteen consecutive years, accumulating over two thousand murders, more than the Afghanistan War in all its years of existence, with over two thousand deceased soldiers in a period of nearly eleven years (2001 up until 2012).

In the state of California, each year, nearly eighteen years more than two thousands murders occurred because of an ongoing war of gangs. Some years recorded staggering numbers, unbelievably doubled two times worse than the Afghanistan War alone, with numbers topping and reaching such high peaks, massively out of control, three thousand, peaking that number ten times within a decade. And four thousand was documented as the highest murder rates to ever peak at such high magnitudes on a scale ratio. No other state has come nowhere near to California, besides Texas, with forty-four consecutive years, with over nearly one thousand murders per year. New York State averages nearly over one thousand murders per year for thirty consecutive years. Chicago averages one thousand murders for nineteen consecutive years. These numbers are staggering!

Texas proves that the bigger the state, the bigger the capitals, the greater the killings. I guarantee that if you search for yourself, you will discover that in Vietnam, nearly 58,138 estimated U.S soldiers died. Research how many murders per state on America soil occurs because of senseless gang violence. I went back as far as the 1960s when less than seven hundred murders occurred per state per year because of the unity and Civil Rights movement. You can compare the events, time, and people of the 1960s with the change and elements of the 1980s as murder rates tripled. Find all the puzzle pieces that caused this tragedy. Know and discover in your own opinion what happened. How the factors I mention will give you so many clues if you read carefully. Then you will discover history's deepest secrets. There are so many deceased, young, fallen black men, casualties of war, heartbroken families. Mothers lose two or three sons or daughters to gang violence to the point of no return. Something has to be done. Families packed up their things. The seniors become innocent bystanders in this hurl of gunfire. Even casualties resulted in many deaths of the elderly, model citizens of our communities, causing an uproar to the point that they became very afraid to speak out loud about the senseless murders, hiding in their homes and lying on the floors when the shooting begins. The city was under siege. The silence was detrimental. The motto was, "Hear nothing, see nothing, know nothing at all." It was the only way to live in peace while minding your own business. You seem to live long avoiding stray bullets from flying through your home and avoiding cocktails from burning down your home, if you were found or known for volunteering vital hood information "What happens in the hood stays in the hood." Some people were known to get hurt really bad. People learned that talking to the cops—normally after they had gotten what they needed from you such as vital information, without any concern as regards protecting their reliable brief witness, obtaining any such title known as an informant or police assistant, in a neighborhood watch program—could cause you your life, leaving you high and dry labeled as the neighborhood rat. It is that easily to result in becoming the newest target. How ironic it is when the coroner would be dispatched to pick up a poor and Good Samaritan that the cops left out on a limb while requesting someone to stand up and come forward and not sit quietly watching such brutal and senseless crimes, once building up the courage and initiating oneself in such a forbidden act of suicide. After this cop's eight-hour shift was over, he returned home to his wife and children in great suburbia with a murder rate of two per year. Unfortunately, the Good Samaritan met his demise while living in the concrete jungle, unable to flee, stuck in between a rock and a hard place with no escape, putting his own life on the limb, giving up vital information against the hyenas of the concrete jungle, becoming a feast in no time; and you know the stories of hyenas. They eat thrown bones and all, devouring all flesh and evidence. And all it takes are a few seconds for a cop to arrive too late or not too soon enough; and a witness is speaking out, trying to assist the cop who doesn't understand the rules of the concrete jungle because of the facts he only works a shift of eight hours and he goes home to his family while the people that are prisoners of war live their day in and day out. Hostage to a situation out of control is our gang land. During shifts of work with all the cruelty of diverse people, criminal elements, and high-stake murders occurring, does a cop fight crime with a flashlight in hand or with weapon on deck? Living in the concrete jungle, it takes seconds for a cop to lose focus and become a statistic. In those same seconds, an unarmed man is assaulted and threatened by hostile armed groups of criminals. How does this man deal with a situation with no choice, placed in the same moment and event as the fallen officer? In seconds, this man shall encounter the same doom that the fallen slain officer endured at the hands of the criminals that disruptively approached this man who doesn't have any choices. It's dark. There's not a soul or human in sight. You help this lonely, helpless man that is about to become a statistic to the bloody hands of this criminal group and cop killer, all alone, scared, with no phones in sight. Yelling out loud for help will only make things much worse. He has no choice while being confronted by this four-man crew, with the cop killer yielding forth a weapon in hand, threatening to murder this man if he doesn't empty out his pockets and give up all his belongings to the four-man criminal crew. This scared man's only purpose is to return home safely. Little did this menacing thug crew know days prior, while out shopping, the old man met a merchant of some sort. This merchant was selling all sorts of items at a discount rate, from watches to hats, belts, and many different items of value. Out of nowhere, the merchant pulled out a small firearm and offered to sell it to this old man for only $250. The old man thought of how dangerous it had become over the years with the emergence of the Crips and Bloods; and just recently, maybe a few days ago, a cop had been shot down in cold-blooded murder in the streets. While pursuing a suspect through a dark alley, the cop was subsequently murdered. At this cheap retail price, the old man figured, living in a hostile environment, it wouldn't hurt him any to buy this six-shot .44 magnum, just in case things got a bit feisty in this concrete jungle. After all, during a few tours in Vietnam, he was highly trained to deal with any sort of weapons. The old man gave up his wallet to the four-man criminal crew and the cop killer whose attributes of murdering a cop was unrevealed. The young cop killer rambled through the old man's wallet. He counted three hundred and fifty-nine dollars along with some coins, but the young cop killer was not happy with the large amount of funds he scored, which the amount would be evenly split among his four-man crew. The young man, holding the gun, pointing it at the old man, seemed to want more than just cash. He seemed to taste blood after murdering the cop many days earlier. His heart had turned cold as ice. Like a man possessed, the old man looked into the young man's eyes, and he could see death in this young man's eyes. The old man hadn't seen a look like that in a man's eyes since his last tour in Vietnam, while encountering Vietnamese who were strung out on opium. They were pushing forth an early death. This young man obtained the same distorted blank look of being lost and out of his mind, with murder and rage in his heart. While pointing the gun at the old man, he fired a shot above the old man's head with the .38 he held in hand. The four-man crew began yelling, "Shoot the old ass man! Shoot him." He had five more shots left. The old man pleaded for his life but was plotting on handling the situation without hurting anyone, resulting in any deaths, because he suffered severe nightmares from enduring a deadly tour in Vietnam that resulted in many lost lives at his hands. So he had no problem with killing or taking a life if it meant protecting his own. It was just the things that happened after he had killed someone and living with so much guilt was sometimes unbearable, not knowing if you were going to be punished to endure a hell because what you thought was right for your country's beliefs was all so wrong. The old man pleaded with the young man, saying, "I can see death in your heart." His crew was shouting, "Kill him now!" He fired two more rounds, striking the old man in the right shoulder, barely missing the second shot, skinning the old man with the second round discharged. The old man grunted out loudly in pain, "Young man, don't make this mistake." The young man urged the old man to hush up and die slow. The crazed four-man crew continued shouting altogether, "Kill him!" Simultaneously, the young man squeezed one more shot off, while pointing the gun directly at the center of the old man's forehead. But the young man's gun finally misfired. Somehow it was jammed. Some unknown divine power had intervened. Now the olden man said, "How will you be able to live with yourself? If you kill me, you will have to kill me over and over again in your nightmares. And that, my son, is a horrible pill to swallow. Are you able to deal with such deadly attributes that come back to haunt you?" He became uncertain of what the old man had said, dazed and confused, plagued by the mind-altering chemical that took full control of the mind with distorted thought and a chemically induced high. One could imagine the drugs this young man abused took complete control of his better judgment.

The young man became enraged. The older man grew restless because of his newer gunshot wounds. With his life on the line, it became apparent that the unthinkable had to be done. Either you could become prey or transform into the predator, reversing the odds. "Dog eat dog" flashed back into his deadly Vietnam-killing mode, as the young man fiddled with the weapon. His crew is encouraging him to commit mayhem. The old man, already injured from the gunshot wounds, finally decided that he had all that he could stand. His words were falling on deaf ears. The pain was very intense. Time seemed to come to a standstill. The young man raised his weapon and fired once more. The old man was hurled to the ground as the velocity of the bullet had sent him stumbling backward. All in one motion, the old man reached unto his waistband unexpectedly and pulled out the bright and shining blue steal .44 magnum. While falling to the ground and landing, he bent into a fetus-type position, breaking his fall and shielding the weapon from being exposed. The old man pulled the firearm, pointing it, aiming and firing at the young crazed man. The young man was in dismay, trying to figure out how this old man had obtained such a large weapon without any suspicion at all. The loud crackling boom of the first two rounds caught everyone's attention, surely striking the young man in the testicles, blowing off his set of balls sack. Clint Eastwood would have been very proud. From the outside, looking in this matter, it had been carried out Dirty Harry style. Things went from "Peace or Bullets." Unfortunately, the young man dropped his weapons after firing numerous rounds, dispensing a few rounds into the old man's shoulder. After falling and gathering his self, the old man was able stabilize the situation and took full control. Upon dropping the weapon to the ground, the young crazed man was in so much pain. The young man screamed for dear life as he groped his testicles, trying to find where they had rolled off. He searched around but without any luck. He couldn't locate them in their usual spot. The young man searched around on the ground, trying to find his balls, which had been blown to smithereens with such a large-caliber hand weapon. Oblivious that he had dropped his own weapon, he was more concerned about where his balls had landed. One of the members of the four-man crew had charged toward the .38 special that was lying in the pool of blood. The young man was bleeding out excessively fast. In anger, his crew reached for the weapon. The old man discharged three carefully fired shots, hitting all three of the remaining men with precision and pure accuracy. Moans and grunts rippled throughout the corridor. All the men lie bleeding, effusively doubting themselves for dealing with an old man that had dealt the pain back to them the same way they were used to issuing it out. For once, they were the ones lying in the pools of blood, torching and dreadful in pain, crying out in harmony, "Please someone call 911. Help! Please help us. Call the cops. Please." One of the so lucky criminal crew members, who went running off hobbling due to his chubby figure, he ran extremely slow; nonetheless, he was injured shot in the leg one of the few lucky ones. He had to retrieve assistance for his crew that had been annihilated by one old man and the luck of draw. Thanks to old reliable Clint Eastwood and the powers that was .44 that proves that peace is much more relaxing than inflicting pain of forcing bullets as a result of implicating the magnitude of an old-fashioned ass whipping!

"Sometimes drastic measures are required to beget positive results." Men of peace choose not war but are masters of war while not indulging in useless or wasted antics to cause harm. Force a man of peace into the battlefield and observe how easy a man of peace can revert back into a killing machine to be reckoned with. To know peace, you have to suffer casualties of war. Pushed to the limits or in the brink of war, a man of peace will become willing to win it at all cost thinkable, with resilience and relentless efforts to persevere his dominant status quo. Peace is kings manship.

The innovated, new three-strike law was initiated during the early 1990s and is now in full effect. Now the saying that was profound during the heyday of gun play drive and murder, which most gangsters usually stated: "I'll kill. You do seven years and come home. Piss on your grave then kill some of your family. Do seven more years and call it a job. But no thanks to the new and improved swing batter. Batter swing! Strike 1, strike 2, strike 3. You're out."

The politicians had become enraged with all the brutality. At times, most shootings were unreported when no one was killed. Assaults with deadly weapons were at an all-time high. Numerous wounded individuals went unreported. Some murders, because of the alarming rate of homicide, had to be swept under the carpet to protect image, covered up, and fabricated secretly. A murder rate was decreased. Homicide rates were erased to save face and to prevent the American people from fearing to visit a city in rage, becoming afraid to migrate, scaring the tourist away from visiting, which affects the currency of money flowing into the "City of Angeles." We couldn't even get a fare bid for the Olympics after being rewarded in 1984. That would be the final year that we had achieved something worth that magnitude. Besides, it didn't matter to the City of Arrogance, Championships, and Angeles. We had the 1988 World Series Champs in the Dodgers, Magic and Kareem, and the World Champions Lakers. Who cared? With the rise of senseless crimes, bank robberies became the biggest crime committed. The Wild, Wild West was full in effect. Car Jacking for Dayton's 100 hundred spokes rims was like the biggest fad. Every criminal-minded or gang-affiliated thug brought some $1,000 100 spokes, and so many lives were lost because some bloodthirsty hoodlum was out head hunting for a feast to get paid and catch a nigga slipping for them things, meaning 100 spokes Dayton's. So many elements existed in the streets, which increased the murder rates, indulging in the everyday life of living and being either Crips or Bloods. This meant you were fearless and in the midst of riding, putting in work, carjacking, bank robberies. Every day, high-speed chases occurred somewhere around you or on televisions. Massive amounts of gun play and shootings occurred. The guessing game of name:. If you name that tune, gunshots were the melody. Your purpose was to name the caliber of gun that was discharged. These are crews of infamous stick-up artist who only targeted big-time drug dealers, the smarter guys who were enrolled in college but more gruesome with a chimp on their shoulder to prove their macho bravado. They were skilled criminals despite their enrollment in school, seeking to obtain college degrees and prove how down they were despite the perception of being called bookworms. A knew fad, a criminal art, was born. It was called home invasion around the time this new crime flourished. It really pushed forward the three-strike law. The Bloods and Crips begin to think robbing just blacks was senseless when the results usually equaled a few hundreds of dollars. Unlike any other gang in existence, the Crips and Bloods were do or die and believed in getting rich or dying while trying. Even the females Cripeletes and Bloodetes lived up to this so-called true G-code during the early '80s and late '90s, setting high standards for all criminal blacks of so-called gangs across the entire United States of LA, from East Coast to the West Coast LA to New York. The movie *Set It Off* was based on a group of female Cripeletes following the footsteps of their O/gee Home Boys from their neighborhood and the large crime wave of bank robberies that launched throughout the city. Being Crips or Bloods in *The City of Angels*, it was a million ways to get paid without a doubt. When certain guys chose not to stake out banks, Nix Check, cashing joints became targets. No place was safe. If money is kept inside a safe, it was due to be robbed. If a word leaked out that your home included a safe, then you became a quick feast, a target on the menu. So many groups were venturing out to the greater suburbia areas of Beverly Hills and Hollywood. If you remember, a string of robberies occurred, which launched the famous lose your chain lose your manhood that rap stars lived by. The rules of engagement of California created this mass hysteria where most rappers were on top of the pile. The movie *Stars Sports*'s figures such as football and basketball players flossed throughout the city, not knowing the intensity of the hyenas, the high stakes that they were willing to take. Once it was mentioned that jewelers would buy jewelry, these mega figures wore these 50,000 chains that was the easiest so-called lick in the world innovated in the city of stars, bright light and sunshine. Jewelry stores were targeted. No place was safe from the infamous Bloods and Crips. The only problems were identifying a prolific star and catching him slipping.

Many stars, actors, sports figures, and rappers were victimized in one state alone during the heyday, when chain snatching from prolific figures was innovated. Sometimes during the heist, some stars usually stated, "Do you know who I am?" This resulted in someone being fatally shot, trying to use their fame to prevent a mugging. Prove a point of do you know who I am. Gang activities reached so many boiling points, spreading into Hollywood. Gang members begin to think outside the box. They figured out that so many white families didn't trust in bank accounts, opening saving accounts and trust funds for their children, college careers, and because of the fact that so many millionaires and white families were so close to reaching the 0.25 of a million-dollar spot. While in the ghetto, hoods are struck with poverty and hunger, staring and looking at Hollywood and Beverly Hills from the outside. Many of the Bloods and Crips wanted to seek revenge for all the wrongs in their life. And in his twisted thought of making amends with all the crimes he committed against his people, he decided to go all in, all out. The one thing that the Crips and Bloods have is the motive that stands firm, do or die, the code they truly lived by willing to be the true epitome of the thug slash gangster, not afraid to venture outside his own backyard and inflict the same violence and dread dealt in the ghettos, giving white suburbia a brief slice or taking his slice of American apple pie with some whip cream.

Please. Thank you very much. Rumors spread like viruses when the local neighborhood's small-arm drug dealer in days surges from small dude on the block to big man on the campus, with a few birds in the mix and a—brand new Low Rider along with a cheap clean bucket of some sort, maybe a 1985 Cutlass, Regal, Caprice, Monte Carlo; a newly found pocket full of money netting nearly 100,000 dollars, split among a group of two, thanks to the crime of home invasion in white suburbia. High-profiled crimes in effect, the entire neighborhood knew the methods of the come up. The youth are younger; aspiring up and coming little soldiers want in. Some guys are good at what they do using brains and patients, but the youth always look and listen. But somehow impatient, they forget the learn part. Once they begin to scout targets, things become very hostile. Things get sloppy, and the net worth usually not much because they include so many unloyal figures that end up ruining everything, getting everyone caught committing a useless shooting resulting in turning a simple burglary into a 187 murder with the dumbest statement in world history because during a robbery, she has seen your face stupid. Ever heard of a ski mask? Have you ever heard of decrease your sentence? Why turn a simple five years into twenty-five years of life jail sentence just because some young uncontrollable is too anxious to prove he can shoot someone! Idiot's that donot think instead reacting on impulse and bad nerves, big mouth of the south with an agenda to tell the whole wide world about his caper's loose lips and talkative. Thus, upon his poor preplanned subplot, guys like him become pure examples for the masses to illustrate what becomes of foolish men who don't carefully think out their plans while committing useless crimes, t not considering to be careful and thoughtful of human life and talking just too much. Examples are carefully conducted in the same fashion during the Wild, Wild West. A man is hung in order to illustrate how other up and coming careless bank robbers that are unruly unjust deploy carelessness, costly mistakes, when dealing with the most evil-minded assailants. The increase skill set in obtaining massive increased cash flow creates a lack of gun control of heavy superior fire power during the heyday of warfare. Money was pleasant, but wars were imminent and more sufficient than cash to your average street thugs Crips or Bloods. Your weapon was your money maker. If you had weapons by no means during the days of superior supreme cutting-edge warfare, your weapon was like a sword considered to a knight. You should never be caught without your armor, less you volunteered to face annihilation. If you were deeply involved in strategic wars like playing chess, you obtained the cash in order to invest in producing a secure protected front line while anointing and choosing soldiers carefully in order to increase cash flow, creating supreme teams of high-caliber, quiet, and discreet soldiers of fortune, ready to engage in all activities. While keeping enemies at bay, transforming young boys into elite warriors, once the cash flow increases, so does the artillery and gun play.

No Independence Day, but with lots of fireworks, like the Fourth of July; and if you came from where I come from, things are done up close and personal. If you lived in the concrete jungle, or even worked there as law enforcement, you understand thoroughly the words I mention. "Thus applying the statement, the enemy of my enemy is my foe, and I'll kill them both." This is what you will see in many hoods who have engaged in these types of wars: wall bang, gang graffiti, the encrypted words "ANY-BODY KILLA!" Drugs play a significant role as regards supplying relentless amounts of artillery, and it helps quench the thirst of wanting and needing. Truth being said, in the hands of a social psychopath who is buried knee deep in these types of all-out warfare, he becomes consumed by the demons of destruct and destroy; therefore, the more the gain, the plenty the profit. The weaponry increases, going from old six-shooters to fully automatics. When the weapon supply increases, so do the malicious violent attacks. The murder statistics rise, families are torn to shreds, as these warriors clash in a battle of the titans. No one is protected, not even the boys in blue whose sole duty is to serve and protect. They have even been targets, fair game. As history has been documented, the proof is in the pudding. Not only is it a known fact that cops would wait for the gunfire to cease, giving the assailants opportunity to flee the scene. The cops were doing their jobs. It was just only one factor that changed the odds. They were not highly equipped for a situation that involved so many high-powered weapons and assailants simultaneously discharging artillery, sounding like thunder crackling through the skies, mimicking drums being beaten repeatedly, never ending, almost everlasting gunfire as your heart race and pound to the beat. I always said that if i was a cop, I know I would rather dodge a bullet today and be able to talk about it tomorrow. The one second it takes a cop to respond to an emergency call, a life can be destroyed and become obsolete while they sit in their vehicles, waiting for the gunfire to cease. What am I supposed to do? Lie down and die willingly without a fighting chance? Does a cop come to the most violent crime-infested hood with a flashlight and a badge? If having a gun to defend my life is wrong, I don't want to be politically right. Like a Master Card, I'd rather be caught with it than without it! I don't consider shook cops to be disgraced, just survivors of their environment. After the Hollywood bank robbery shootout, the standoff exposed the inferiority that had been concealed for years. Cops have always complained to their superiors how out gunned they were. That day marked a new beginning. Every squad car was equipped with assault rifles to match the fire power of the gangs. Remember, at the beginning, I said gangs are like AIDS and cancer. No matter what you do to treat it, it never seems to go away. It is hidden, undetected. It adapts to the change in the body or environment. Then, suddenly, it comes back stronger, exposing itself and slowly devouring its victim, spreading fast and rapidly.

There are levels that each gang affiliate operates on. By levels, I mean associates in his methods of crimes. He will pursue many illegal skills in order to progress. Skills can mean anything from simple burglaries to homicides. Whatever he excels at would become the crime of his true profession. The edge, the danger, the thrill of the hunt is like being a junky with a dying need, a thirst that is never quenched. The more stripes you take, the more you become consumed like a fiend. For this adrenaline rush, nothing can compare. This is the same medicine that presidents have pursued for hundreds of years. The taste of conquering and destroying your opposition, the satisfaction, is overwhelming—when you gain ground on your enemy, out pacing him, out thinking him, lashing out with every blow, connecting with precise accuracy with every lethal strike, effectively damaging, breaking the enemy down slowly like a prize fighter who unleashes devastating, crippling body shots that he mix it up so he can attack and unleash the home run hit. It's all war. Does a prize fighter before a bout train for a ballerina dance? Or does he prepare for war? Demolish your opponent until he retreats and surrender. Outguessing his every calculated thought and forcing his judgment until he destroys himself with every move he makes becomes fatal. Realize that not every soldier is born a soldier, just participants, like a draft that's held in sports that groom the best, elite, prolific players that are going to be the next generation of either average players, stars, or superstars. Now, every decade or so, here comes a player that's on everybody's radar: the Magic, Jordan, Birds, Lebron, and Kobe of the game. And when they play, they shoot the lights out. It's a known fact that somebody's kid is going to get drafted in the hood, and he's going to be some gang's number 1 draft pick. This innocent born child will grow up one day, living in his environment, becoming his environment. He will be groomed in a lifestyle of chaos and violence. He and his environment will apparently become conjoined as one, a killing machine, a force to be reckoned with. And the more gruesome he becomes, the more the scouts are going to recruit this young player in the gang to shoot the lights out on their side of the ball. Of course, every young and upcoming player wants the spotlight, the fame, and the glory (stripes). He wants to write history like every other "great street legend" before his time. The gangs always have this bigger-than-life untouchable person, a legend of the hood who is admired by masses (hated by many, respected by all). They practice daily to pursue this quest of rage and inflict unthinkable amounts of violence, transforming into this uncontrollable beast. In his own world, this is all he has ever known. This is his way of communicating as regards respect. He knows no other way because every soldier has his own personnel quest because of his unfortunate circumstances that life has dealt for him or just because of pure plain old desires to rebel against his home and disciplinary moral teachings that he rejects because this rogue life is more intriguing and has a greater challenge. Because the edge is more exciting, he chooses death without a vivid continence or fear of signing his own contract of death. His mind has been contaminated relentlessly by scouts. Some kids have no chance or choice every day. They take a walk to school or to the store for their parents. They become victims of gang altercations. Either they stay on the wrong side of the tracks or they are directly in the center. The few good kids who try to avoid the scouts, the gang members, and their violence have a way to distract the good kids and set their course off track, leading them into the wrong direction, forcing their hands, giving them no escape or multiple choices to make decisions. They become threatened and cornered, becoming prey to unusual torment. They are stuck in between a rock and a hard place. They fight the temptation of becoming initiated, but the gang's choke hold proves over and over to be a full threat too powerful to flee from. So a kid who is taught virtues is conquered to retreat into submission. Most likely, he will choose the side that inflicted the less amount of humiliation and brute embarrassments. No matter how they became, what matters is who they are now! "America's Menace II Society"! A monster is now born again, even adopting a new name that he intends to glorify as if he was Greek or Roman, a modern-day gladiator who seeks to have his name marveled with every breath. Even after his death, when he has passed and entered the afterlife, his entire life is only for this moment, to create chaos so that his name is remembered by the masses and he is not forgotten, even in death, fossilized on the walls as the hood's fabulous, with spray-painted graffiti. May our legend live on. Troy had Achilles. Rome had Alexander the Great. Germany had Hitler. Chicago had Al Capone. So understand, yes, every hood has a person of great significant value in their own eyes. The bad guys of before have paved the way for the bad guys of the future because our perfect world doesn't show any remorse or love for the oppressed people of its society, which creates splinter cells of rebellions like a Robin Hood in the hood. The fat gets fatter, which is the rich; the skinny people die worldwide, which are the poor people. Everything that created a notorious Crips, Blood, Gd, BPS, LK, SUR13, Whatever you have become, the true plan is to destroy a specific race and culture. Our history consists of great leaders and studies how the ones who spoke great words. had the power to deliver the message with great force and deadly power. They were cerebral thinkers with a divine destiny in their favor. They were ordained to do these things in order to put a stamp on historical events. In death, they would shape the world. "Sometimes you're a nobody until somebody kills you." Everything has a ripple effect. When something dies out, something else begins to happen. That is what we know as evolution: every event from Harriet Tubman to Rosa Parks; Martin Luther King; Malcolm X; even the demise of the Black Panther movement;. the assassination of John F. Kennedy, Robert F. Kennedy, Martin L. King, Malcolm X, Panther Party members, and many unknown KKK victims that were brutally hung, torched, and murdered. This demonstrates the hate that is involved against the black race. The great question we all would love to know is why? Do those people who so dearly hate blacks? Why? Tell me the answer. Please! Tell us if we are so inferior to the white race! Why hate us if you are superior, supposedly? Does anyone know why? If we are so ignorant, dumb, why give whites a head start and forbid and outlaw coloreds who are not able to read? And if a colored does, he risks being murdered. That's a telltale sign of a person with an inferiority complex! As slaves, we were trained to have no dignity of self. We were separated and maimed of family values. They took one nigger and put him in the house and put the other in the field, creating a house nigger with privileges and a field nigger with harsh, strenuous labor, sometimes making the house slave beat the field slave, causing friction between the two. In manipulation, this form of black-on-black crime was created. This physiological unfair abuse affected and molded the makeup of the black man for four hundred years of punishment by all means of torture, the same way a monkey would be placed in an astronaut suit, be experimented on, and be sent to the moon. The black man was a target purpose to destroy and deplete the Negroid seed with long-term jeopardy plan, well thought out and executed by scholars and opposite colors of the black race. The psychological effects of long-term abuse programming, the perfect slave race, the black man, a subject of experimental purposes. In 2012, more than four hundred years later, we define the black race demeanor, attitude, his surroundings, the elements in his surroundings. The ratio numbers compared with any other race. People are dying from naturally caused deaths, considered accidents, sicknesses, diseases without cures that affected the most. Don't fall for most of what you hear. Racism never died. It's in camouflage, stronger and covered. Pay attention. Think places to snipe and pick off someone you dislike. This is the place of power. Those positions are where they have climbed, and we must also adjust. If they have evolved, we must evolve to defend and protect the people from racism. Those things have shaped a race that has persevered, but every now and then, a rosebud grows out of the concrete that we bury ourselves in. We will never forget what our people had to suffer, no matter how much we hate ourselves, no matter how much we kill each other. The fact is we came so far and we were stripped of our moral identity that we ourselves have set back more than four hundred years. We hang each other now. We enslave each other. All any racist clan member have to do is watch the news and celebrate. We have blacks that are placed in positions of power, who works in a society that secretly funded a new method of destroying a race. It only proves that the field nigger syndrome and the house nigger syndrome continues to live within us today, while an evolved and more sophisticated clan is operating behind the scenes, granting the field nigger with limited powers and blockades. Just in case he chooses to assist his fellow black man, his chain will be snatched. Even though he has some power, he will always be reminded who he really is. When he operates outside, there is a line of defense. The clan is not extinct. They are more powerful than ever. They gave up their hoods and sheets and evolved. That hate, which is so powerful, never dies. It never died Do you remember those marches of nonviolence? Did you see those large crowds of old and young white people who stoned Dr. Martin Luther King? Did you see the hate in their eyes? Did they all die of some horrific excruciating death? The black people who endured such hate are still around to speak about it. Where are the whites who threw the stones? The truth is they are living, and the hate is strong as ever in their secret society. It is much more convenient to operate behind the scenes, without the unwanted attention causing a catastrophic uproar because now these evolved niggers shoot back. The clan has a more political structure. They operate in various fields now, undetected, off the radar. With greater goals and missions, they hide their true identity by public acts of goods deeds toward the people. Remember, everything that glitters is not gold, and everything offered as a gift is a hand extended with cruel intentions. The upside-down smile is usually a frown behind it. I hate to say it, but some whites have some cruel unusual intentions for the black race, if we don't stop saying and denying the facts, lying to ourselves to secure job positions, and our white friends who only like you because you act white. We better wake up out of this foolish lie we are living. Check the schools, hospitals, jails, the streets, and political places. Our own people are turning on us and doing a job for the clan men. Believe it or not, hired hands are working, accepting payoffs, committing murders for their masters. You may ask where the facts. Look at the damn. statistics. People of color are dying in hospitals for unknown reasons and some hidden facts or unrevealed cover-up. And black people are so afraid. Some have stood, but they are afraid to come forth with what they have seen. Intimidated, they hide, knowing about the mass plan to make the black race extinct. Black people, we search for only a few days, then we say I didn't see anything. We give up, and the plan continues while we are gone home forgetting about everything we were told by some patient or criminal because someone had said he's medicated, he's crazy, he's a criminal. His word is not justified or competent. Stop allowing unjust, demoralizing people tell you when to stand and sit down, allowing you to succumb and accept, enduring genocide of your people because a white says he is not worth anything or life. The truth is that's deception; and if you fall for it, you just might as well be the damn clan yourself because you surely will be next. Stop watching and going along, playing God with your own people's lives. After all, how many whites have you envisioned with your own eyes that have endured the same inflicting torment that we indirectly cause upon each other by thinking that all white men like black men? They'll rather kill you. This isn't racism. I speak just truth when a black tells the white man's nature and hidden agendas. Behind the scene, that black then is labeled a racist for speaking golden hidden realities. Black people wake up, and the Judas of the people wipe them out. Once a traitor, always a traitor. Evaluate him or her, isolate them, and find out why they turned on their people. Some had no choices, forced, but the one who do it for money, and that's it. He is no longer a black man. They truly want to annihilate the race. Sometimes the hate is so strong, no matter how much makeup they put on, no matter how much they smile, no matter how much good they do, their eyes always tell the truth that is within. "The eyes are the windows of the soul." Don't be astonished or fooled. Your new Klux Klux Klan can be your ex-president, a person of political power who passes bills of rights, law enforcement. Doctors, district attorneys, teachers, judges. Who runs the show now? Think about it. We have a black president who was selected! How much do you think that he will be allowed to do? There is always a power behind power. Believe Obama was ordained to be a president, some unknown plot that is in the making, and the truth will come to light. Every move is manipulated for the people or against the people. Sometimes we become so wise we are dumb. The greatest illusion performed is deception right before your eyes, with a wool pulled over your head. We search for the sophisticated broad view of deception of people. All along, it's the smaller views that are untouched. As long as one person has been allowed to obtain certain positions, they forget who they are fighting for. Their purpose and view become tainted because of their new lifestyle and profits of gain. They lose sight of their true purpose. Did Jesus dwell with the rich? Anything in the same category as gangs can consume your soul when you let it overpower your outlook of life, causing you to blemish within. You have been marked by the beast, by that which you vaguely allow to consume your soul. Satan has many methods. He knows the desires in men hearts. In a struggle for your soul, all you have to do is say yes, represent anything that is not right by God. The word is written to teach the ways so that you may identify the fog and see through it.

HOMICIDE MURDERS AND YEARS COMMITTED IN LA

Year	Murder	Year	Murder
1967	281	1987	812
1968	349	1988	736
1969	377	1989	874
1970	394	1990	983
1971	427	1991	1,025
1972	501	1992	1,092
1973	491	1993	1,077
1974	481	1994	850
1975	556	1995	838
1976	517	1996	707
1977	574	1997	566
1978	678	1998	419
1979	817	1999	420
1980	1,028	2000	542
1981	877	2001	605
1982	844	2002	646
1983	818	2003	526
1984	757	2004	515
1985	777	2005	490
1986	831	2006	478

Chicago Murder Rate
from Years 1991 to 2011

Year	Murder
1991	928
1992	943
1993	855
1994	931
1995	828
1996	796
1997	761
1998	704
1999	643
2000	633
2001	667
2002	656
2003	601
2004	453
2005	451
2006	471
2007	448
2008	513
2009	459
2010	436
2011	433

Illinios State Murder Rate
from Years 1960 to 2011

Year	Murder	Year	Murder
1960	489	1986	1,023
1961	492	1987	967
1962	537	1988	991
1963	523	1989	1,051
1964	572	1990	1,182
1965	551	1991	1,300
1966	745	1992	1,322
1967	793	1993	1,332
1968	893	1994	1,378
1969		1995	
1970	1,066	1996	1,179
1971	1,079	1997	1,096
1972	985	1998	1,008
1973	1,163	1999	939
1974	1,319	2000	891
1975	1,179	2001	982
1976	1,161	2002	961
1977	1,109	2003	895
1978	1,108	2004	780
1979	1,203	2005	770
1980	1,205	2006	780
1981	1,205	2007	752
1982	1,005	2008	790
1983	1,112	2009	773
1984	1,033	2010	704
1985	927	2011	721

CALIFORNIA MURDER RATE FROM YEARS 1960 TO 2011

Year	Murder	Year	Murder
1960	616	1986	3,038
1961	605	1987	2,924
1962	657	1988	2,936
1963	673	1989	3,158
1964	740	1990	3,553
1965	880	1991	3,859
1966	868	1992	3,921
1967	1,039	1993	4,096
1968	1,150	1994	3,703
1969	1,386	1995	3,531
1970	1,376	1996	2,916
1971	1,642	1997	2,579
1972	1,791	1998	2,171
1973	1,862	1999	2,005
1974	1,985	2000	2,079
1975	2,209	2001	2,206
1976	2,220	2002	2,395
1977	2,515	2003	2,407
1978	2,611	2004	2,392
1979	2,952	2005	2,503
1980	3,411	2006	2,485
1981	3,143	2007	2,260
1982	2,779	2008	2,142
1983	2,639	2009	1,972
1984	2,717	2010	1,809
1985	2,770	2011	1,792

New York State Murder Rate
from Years 1965 to 2011

Year	Murder	Year	Murder
1965	836	1989	2,246
1966	882	1990	2,605
1967	996	1991	2,571
1968	1,185	1992	2,397
1969	1,324	1993	2,420
1970	1,444	1994	2,016
1971	1,823	1995	1,550
1972	2,026	1996	1,350
1973	2,040	1997	1,093
1974	1,919	1998	924
1975	1,996	1999	903
1976	1,969	2000	952
1977	1,919	2001	960
1978	1,820	2002	909
1979	2,092	2003	934
1980	2,228	2004	889
1981	2,166	2005	874
1982	2,013	2006	921
1983	1,958	2007	801
1984	1,786	2008	836
1985	1,683	2009	781
1986	1,907	2010	868
1987	2,016	2011	774
1988	2,224		

MICHIGAN STATE MURDER RATE FROM YEARS 1965 TO 2011

Year	Murder	Year	Murder
1965	378	1989	993
1966	415	1990	971
1967	560	1991	1,009
1968	669	1992	938
1969	770	1993	933
1970	831	1994	927
1971	942	1995	808
1972	999	1996	722
1973	1,096	1997	759
1974	1,186	1998	721
1975	1,086	1999	695
1976	1,014	2000	669
1977	853	2001	672
1978	972	2002	678
1979	834	2003	612
1980	940	2004	643
1981	861	2005	629
1982	827	2006	713
1983	910	2007	676
1984	979	2008	554
1985	1,018	2009	628
1986	1,032	2010	580
1987	1,124	2011	613
1988	1,009		

Florida State Murder Rate from Years 1965 to 2011

Year	Murder	Year	Murder
1965	518	1989	
1966	612	1990	1,379
1967		1991	1,248
1968	731	1992	1,208
1969	720	1993	1,224
1970	860	1994	1,165
1971	933	1995	1,037
1972	924	1996	1,077
1973	1,180	1997	1,012
1974	1,190	1998	967
1975	1,130	1999	859
1976	903	2000	903
1977	859	2001	874
1978	949	2002	911
1979	1,084	2003	924
1980	1,387	2004	946
1981	1,522	2005	883
1982	1,409	2006	1,129
1983	1,199	2007	1,201
1984	1,264	2008	1,169
1985	1,296	2009	1,011
1986	1,371	2010	987
1987	1,317	2011	984
1988	1,416		

Texas State Murder Rate from Years 1960 to 2011

Year	Murder	Year	Murder
1970	1,299	1992	2,239
1971	1,383	1993	2,147
1972	1,440	1994	2,022
1973	1,506	1995	1,963
1974	1,652	1996	1,477
1975	1,639	1997	1,327
1976	1,515	1998	1,346
1977	1,705	1999	1,217
1978	1,853	2000	1,238
1979	2,253	2001	1,332
1980	2,392	2002	1,302
1981	2,446	2003	1,422
1982	2,466	2004	1,364
1983	2,239	2005	1,407
1984	2,093	2006	1,384
1985	2,132	2007	1,420
1986	2,258	2008	1,370
1987	1,959	2009	1,330
1988	2,022	2010	1,163
1989	2,029	2011	1,269
1990	2,389		

"The Underworld, Underground Slave City" (Prisoners of War)

This the great escape from Los Angeles, on the run, attempting to avoid capture of this modern-day legalized slavery inside the many California prisons that springs to existence more regularly than colleges, with higher enrollment percentages per ratio. There are many unwilling participants of many diverse ethnic groups. Some are falsely accused of crimes that they had not been fairly treated during trial, and representation was just an antic. Some public-appointed pretender acts as if he's or she's going to defend your rights, all the long with a designed purpose to railroad you in the process.

More blacks and Hispanics' minority groups are subjected as prisoners. They find themselves prisoners of war, confined behind cages, twenty-three hours during a total day's cycle. Menacing as it may seem, some criminals deserve everything that has occurred to them, suffering for offenses or crimes committed against the helpless or defenseless while enduring jail terms. The worse of the worse are not condoned. Even inmates have a respect for conduct and disapproval for men who take advantage of old men and women and rapists of kids. Some criminals were once modest everyday people, tax-paying citizens, with one thought, one mistake that resulted in nearly twenty-five years to life. These moments of anger leading to temporarily insanity could happen to any person. Understand that living in the real outside world, we are all just one simple illogical mistake away from serving thirty-five years. With all the gang activities, the street elements futile with hostility, waiting to devour its prey in self-defense, you can easily receive life. In the state of California, self-defense doesn't exist. A man protecting himself and his family can be sentenced after trial in the same pretense of a murdering, homicidal, heartless maniac.

Some good men sit stacked on the shelves, locked in cages in a factory, branded and counted like cattle, becoming known and identified by the number. A million-dollar profit jailing is a new corporate franchise, a big business. Men sit decaying, facing life-term sentences without the doubt of ever seeing daylight

41

ever again in life. Without political connection and being just the average
Joe, people without financial affordability to pay and provide proper legal
representation, so many men have received maximum terms that may have been
reduced if they were aware of their legal rights or maybe even exonerated. So
many black men have been emancipated after serving more than twenty-five
years in prison, after further evidence was discovered to implicate these men of
their accused crimes. This are mere results of racism and the new evolved Klans
manship in positions of adequate power, which allows them to become secretively
involved in genocide. They will, of course, deny that judges, district attorneys,
correctional officers, police officers, jury, public attorneys, and teachers are all in
this modern-day elite design to deplete the black men from existing. They call it
law, but it's a white law to protect the white race and guarantee them dominance
and control, securing their spot at the top. Do you think any race that has
been involved in some of the most despicable heinous crimes ever committed
involving many wars to reach the top? Do you surely think they would allow one
mixed impure blood of an opposite race rule the kingdom they built through
blood, sweat, and tears? To satisfy and quench the desires to prevent upstaged
pandemonium and rebelling people that are tired and ready to riot as regards
proving a point? One man can move the crowd like Martin L. King, Malcolm X.
The right man can unite the people, creating havoc and a break in the system
felt worldwide, but he must be loyal and honest with the minorities, able to
reach the people with thoughtful knowledge, truth spoken without hiding and
holding back moral expression, and the true facts of the world that media blow
up, programming and feeding the masses. People say we have no leaders. Truth
is, we are all leaders. Together we must reemerge and reclaim our unity because
sometimes when you want something so badly, you have to go out and get it. Take
back what belongs rightfully to you! It's not wrong to speak these facts, finding
out the reasons why we are dying. Stop the finger pointing and join forces in
unity of alleviating self-hatred. We are black and proud! We must start believing
in ourselves, starting with the elders, re-educating the youth about our past, what
the elders endured and suffered, how much was put on the lines. So they won't
forget. Start back demonstrating, marching to end gang violence. The elders
learn not to be afraid or tired, unreluctant to stand on the same corners that the
dealers occupy. I guarantee many youth will stand with you and for you. Remind
them. Tell them what our ancestors endured because they need to hear this from
the mouths of the actual sources, the true history events, up close participants
who were involved in bigotry. We say we have no leaders? All it takes is one man
to create a movement, stirring things up with good moral support from the
people, commitment and support. Don't be afraid of casualties. After all, we have
suffered so much. What more can happen that we haven't endured? Our purpose
is to avoid facing extinction, if we don't take our roles and stand tall before
encountering a pandemic.

Many men in prison have become redeemed, cleansed. Poor righteous teachers, isolated, but they have found liberation and experienced things that no man or woman knows! Behind this big wall, hidden from the eyes of the world outside, politicians fail constantly. They are paid and become settled, only pretending to assist the people. In this underworld city, these men have succumbed to a modern-day form of slavery. Guinea pigs that are hidden, subjects of illegal ill-thought experiments and profitable merchandise, product for retail gain, legal in every condoned political aspect because they are "prisoners of war," who are defaced, believed not to have any morality or human quality. With the lack of support from the people who have obtained legal political position, the inmates are considered scums of the earth or nonfactors, not important, nonhuman in the eyes of the system. As millions of dollars are profited, criminals are well worth the attention, well worth being kept in a cage for eternity. Some men have received life for simple burglary and theft, attempting to feed their poor hungry families. Some are simply attics needing rehab, to treat a diseased state condition. Some men were troublesome during the early '60s and '70s and were strike out for a petition signed in the '90s after they had already been convicted with nearly ten felonies. All it takes is to end up back in prison with life for men who have obtain more than three felony convictions in their past. They are set up tor failure. If they jaywalk and cross the street against a red light, or commit theft of a piece of gum, then they are gone for the rest of their soon-to-be miserable lives, overaged with the development of imminent health problems. They won't make it with a new jail term at age of fifty years old, sentenced to serve twenty-five years to life. Not all inmates are all bad. Actually, more politicians and more citizens are as guilty without morality in their hearts. They kill, lie, and steal in a way that they haven't been caught, only using laws and hidden agendas to be permitted to committing white-collared crimes undetected and at free will. The Knights of the Round Table exist, and even the biggest boss has a boss. He is just the face to relax the people from rebelling, causing havoc and uproar, dismantling an order of control, without the people committed to the government. There is no army to protect the government from foreign invaders. So if they satisfy the people, we become docile while, they discreetly plot to rule and deplete our population! Great numbers that are wiped out allows them to control the people easily with population deduction! The plan is when a man is distracted, watching the left-hand "Obama," distracted with belief persuasion of the crowd, with that, "yes, we can" overcome racism and a liberal speech, Illusion of deception! Keeping the people settled, relaxing the mob before uproar ignites, telling the mass exactly what they want to hear, calming and defusing the population of people who have the true power in numbers and unity. While the right hand is in cover, planning ways to reinvent the massive Jewish extinction committed by Hitler and his German leaders. In the form of minorities replacing the Jews, the prime direct target is the black race! We have been for as long as history can date back. Don't call me racist! Research the facts. Overlook the illusions that assume we have more successful black people. Because more blacks are fortunate, success doesn't eradicate the facts why hate of race existed during Jesus Christ's time! Today's modern times, that same hate consumes people. Understand, some things are just allowed. Use common knowledge!

"UNDERWORLD, UNDERGROUND, PRISON SENTENCE"

Modern-day legalized slavery! Men have no motivation, ties with gang affiliation, unable and unwilling to produce time for nothing else but engagement of war. Even in prison, the black-on-black crime rates are higher than any such activities on the streets, with jailhouse politics. "Prisoners of war"! Pain and punishment increase rival gangs' violent conductive behavior, competing for control of say so! Rights and currency distribution of conversery and cosmetics. Racial lines become limited boundaries, deadly when crossed! Blacks and Hispanics are the dominant ethnic groups in prison. Aryan White Supremacist racist gangs are scarce but dangerous. They usually combat other ethnicities, creating division and conflict among the two playing mediators, more so instigating rivalries with Afro-American and Hispanics because of their lacking numbers. Deception is an vital tool used to their advantage, securing an alliance with the Hispanics, joining forces to combat the Afro-American race. The Aryan White Supremacist gang was known to receive outside help during an upstaged brewing race riot. Outnumbered four to one, the odds were more favorable as an advantage Crips and Bloods began sharpening pencils and toothbrushes, preparing for head-on crash course collisions. While the White Supremacist summoned upon that old Viking spirit, somehow they yielded forth real "six-inch-long knives," turning a simple verbal disagreement and prison brawl into a bloodbath massacre. Thanks to the element of surprise, sixty Afro-Americans were annihilated, repeatedly and brutally stabbed, and chased throughout the prison corridor by only twenty White Supremacists. Afterward, the rumors were spreading throughout the prison. Retaliation was imminent, but what no one could understand is that with such high security levels and metal detectors, how were the Rambo-like swords let inside to cause damage upon the Africans only? How the White Supremacist groups had received real weapons, helping the Hispanics launch a barrage of racial-motivated, full-out attacks on any Afro-American was never solved! California prisons were known for these sort of demographical designed events, promoting riots of racial conflicts, the ultimate warriors colliding in death matches, while wagers were determined what ethnicities would finish victorious and sometimes adding some mischief. The Africans fought two battles on different fronts: convicts and guards. Guards sometime aimed, and by accident with itchy fingers, the trigger was pulled. And some Hispanic or African lie dead on the prison corridors' cement ground! Subsequently, other ethnicities were provided with weaponry to equalize their advantages of survival, and infliction of casualties was tremendous during racially fought prison riots! Even though Africans were less likely to receive any assistance with someone privately supplying them with exceptional superb weaponry, their natural fighting skills disarmed their opponents, knocking other men unconscious. Usually, it was the difference between the living and dying, disregarding the fact that they had been stabbed numerous times, repeatedly. They were forced to fight for survival. Running only caused you your life! "The true gladiators in cages!" "The real animals!" Fighting for survival, life, control, and respect. Inmates graduate into convicts with heavy, durable, long-term sentences. Conflicts erupted. The prison gangs collided simply for no reasons at all. Regular stabbings occur. Riots of racial concern break out! Some are racially motivated, resulting in deaths; and an all-out lockdown occurs, upon having a highly ignited prison war that takes place without any warning or detection. Convicts become great actors, learning to deceive the correctional officers (guards), even when they know an ensuring war is imminent to ignite, erupting into an upscale battlefield of gladiators, yielding forth jail-made shanks and shields of body armor to avoid stabbings. Convicts will not speak one word to tip off the guards. Usually, the commitment to silence is the only way the guards can sense the boiling tensions brewing. Unity among the African American in prison is vital to survival in places where high increased race riots spur, creating a dilemma, the ultimatum to unite and combine all forces to combat ourselves against racist groups who always target Africans in such melee of unethical premonitions, assuming that we will lie down submissively without putting up a fight. We may disagree. We may fight each other, but when it all counts and everything on the line, even some of the women will lay down their lives for their loved ones. After all, we have been laying our lives down every day, when it truly matters. "An African American knows how to take stand in defense for liberation and true justice." "Power to the people!" Putting aside any indifferences that were derived from the streets. Segregated groups are appointed to areas based on race ethnicities and gang involvement. Outside, in the real world, not being able to comply as a productive citizen, you can feel worthless and out of place. In prison, if a normal everyday citizen is incarcerated and he is not involved in gangs, he is considered neutral. It could become very fatal. Rather, he continues on living or dying. The gangs are in control, ruling and running its domain; and "shot callers" are equivalent to the status of the president.

Without disagreeing or rebelling, prisoners become productive, modest citizens in their fields of employment while in prison, inside the underground confinement. Nevertheless, in the real world, the term real world is used because of the nightmarish persona prison implicates! Outside the prison walls, you couldn't pay them a dime to become loyal, modest, conductive citizens contributing to a true worthy cause! Supporting the single struggling black women who have suffered becoming abandoned, forced to endure the world's hardships while raising children, attempting to teach young boys to become men. The underground, underworld is such a dark forbidden mystic nightmare. This dark place is unforgettable. Imagine being sentenced to a living torture zone. Screams echo throughout the misty night when the gates are shut. Grown men moan like little girls, resulting in sexual intimacy, unwilling to partake in homosexual conduct but forced because of the lack of defensive skill developed to fight off such despicable predators that approach you in alarming large groups. A world within a systematic world. Rules are compliant to the men who are determined not to become institutionalized, partaking in animal-like motives and instincts. Thus, it is a place that a man is sentenced to serve life; and if he is an innocent man, imagine the effect that witnessing so much brutality can do to a man, how much he can change. During a man's life, when he was young and consumed with immaturity, the lost years that he committed a senseless, thoughtless crime and was sentenced to life. After serving over fifteen years, a man can be reformed, if he is in the correct facility and refuses to participate in criminal activities and begin to educate himself, obtaining degrees and seeking employment, obtaining trades in which he developed himself into somewhat a citizen in prison! Because of self-education, he discovered knowledge and liberated his mind that had been enslaved because of his immaturity and inability to think outside the lines of thought process. In prison, his mind became emancipated while in flesh he was in prison. Understand that this concept mentioned that men do change for the better and some for the worse. It all depends on the person! Most men, while they were youth without direction and disciplinary actions, grow up in a dysfunctional home. Some poor and struggling mother gave her all, trying her best but failing; while the father, who bailed out, left the mother alone with children to fend as a family without a father figure in their household. In some form or fashion, the father may have grown up fatherless and a victim who succumbed to the same dysfunctional revolving doors of entrapment of a systematic design, orchestrated to devour and demoralize a man, reproducing a "prisoner of war," which the black man has endured and suffered the most of any racial ethnicities!

"Sometimes out of sight, out of mind." While doing time, you have to cast away your entire family and forget about the warm, tender, loving care. It hurts to be in love and sentenced to only a brief term, serving only 365 days within that short period of time. So much can change outside the walls. Environments change Its appearances and people change in personality. Men go in with families and come out with nothing! In just one year, a family can be torn apart and be destroyed, which affects the children and the female companion. She becomes withdrawn, displaced, emotionally distraught, and angry with the man who was abducted and sentenced. The women strike back with resentment and lack of support. Feeling abandoned, the woman returns the feeling by not visiting or writing! Another man emerges out of nowhere, noticing the absence in her home, usually a friend of her husband who sits in prison. A heated affair occurs. Imagine calling home from prison, and in the background, a man's voice echoes. She tries to hold back and fight the moans of passion and intimacy. Hurt and scared in prison and having no control over the ongoing events! She rubs the infidelity in your face. Deeply hurt, you have to accept pain along with the sorrow and time. "Out of sight, out of mind." "You learn to bury your heart in your shoe!"

BACK TO THE HOOD
WITH A VENGEANCE

"Freedom bells ring, emancipated." Receiving two hundred dollars of gate money, you are granted with or without any new skills learned. For better or worse, you are released back into the hood. It's your own agenda and purpose to put together a strong master plan to succeed with many long-term, life-sentenced convicts, who will never come home. They instructed you and persuaded you to not blow this golden opportunity, which they would never get, the chance to smell freedom and taste fresh air. Back in the hood, the same environment that enticed you in your life of crime, more dedicated to serving and supporting your comrades, you neglected your family in the progress and during imprisonment. "Out of sight, out of mind." They distinctively dragged your name through the mud inconspicuously, enviously, and obscenely. They have disrespectfully spit in your face after all the attributions and war fighting against foes, putting your turf on the top of the pile, alone with very little support from fellow affiliates, riding out, putting in work all for the purpose of recognition of the hood, in pursuit of being the best of the best. Betrayal is an unjust and unloyal code of dishonor among thieves! With no true respect, they violate you by sleeping with your women. She was different than the other females. All the others were play toys in the street your fellow affiliates shared and shared alike, taking turns, switching with the so-called local neighborhood rat, a term for the most promiscuous females. But every thug, every gang star, has a special girl. And everyone knows she is the one that remains off limits, no matter what! She is the special one! "Numero uno." The one who he commits his heart to, the true devotion, dedicated to only loving her solely, the one who he prefers to settle down with, to grow old with together, loyally dedicated with one another as a couple unified! After his life of crime is finished, she is the one that he will send to school to enhance her financial status. She's the one who will receive all the profits he gains. She shall be gifted to bear his seed. She is the one he shall go home to every night, sleeping in the same bed, he and her intertwined in relentless passionate love making. He would put his own life in the line of fire to protect her. We know when the cat is away, the mouse will come out to play. Pure disrespect out of all the nine billion men and women on earth, some unloyal and true coward wants to prove that he is the pimp or Mack of the year, violating the rules of the game, dry snitching on you about your deepest secrets, which occurred privately in the jungles of the hood in the battlefield, attempting to gain entry. They tell all the forbidden things that were not ever meant to be spoken—your involvement with other female acquaintances—creating a rip in your relationship and distrust so that it becomes easier for them to persuade your prize, your special hidden trophy, to succumb to their folly! All the while, you sit far and distant in prison, unable to defend your morality and pride. Its principalities involved some lines that are never meant to be crossed, no matter what the cost maybe, even if death is imminent. Being a true and real warrior, you stand alone, elite, because you live by morality and respect for thy allies. No group shall maintain its dominance with such added simplicity of resentment, envy, and egotistical sentimental values that causes a house to fall, divided with disastrous effects. With revenge in heart, the newer enemy involves your own teammates, your own "soldiers of fortune." They have committed the worse crimes among all men, sleeping with another man's property. Rats live like rats! No respect for others, clawing and fighting, never gaining, but always the pest of pestilence, with no pride or respect for the others. Returning home from prison and learning that friends are few and that the closest one to you will do you. You being the first round draft pick, putting that small place in a notable place of recognition, to where it became adequate to go places and receive a pass because no one wanted to engage or rumble because of the respect factor and fear of your gang! You rather have chosen during war to be feared than loved. Giving your team the edge, many members gain refuge in the group, living under the umbrella of protection, while violating, doing damage within, breaking up the stronghold in mischievous mannerism, applying the "rat syndrome" of "we are scandalous." With pride quoting, we can't be trusted. Without honor and pride, a true coward is passive and afraid to inflict that same deception outside the lines in some enemy's hood. Hypothetically speaking, deep within our own lines, our hood, we are strong with loyal, dedicated, honest soldiers of the force, with alternate direct agendas only intended for one purpose—only to decimate and annihilate all enemies. A rat-minded, untrustworthy, snake Judas causes a disease to spread, destroying our invincible, impenetrable walls of protection, deliberately creating publicity stunts for notoriety and deception. Thus, wars are formed inside the lines. A true leader guides by example and creates unity, which creates a team that passes the ball and plays defense, watching each other's backs, committed till death. Victorious with support and righteous communication skills. Violation of one's property, seeking, bragging rights. What does a fool in his folly gain when he causes his team the entire game? Multiple championships, nearly four years in a row. The best team in the paint, the Lamborghini of all cars, then you go from winning rings to just making the Playoffs, from making the Playoffs to not even winning, becoming a public embarrassment to the city, walking around with your head held down. No unity separates the team, and the true snakes and rats think back to what was so powerful and great now has become more like a wasteland of prey. The fools of folly don't stand and tell their stories of their hands being deep down inside the cookie jar, unable to man up, taking full accountability of one's deception and foulness that crippled and sunk the *Titanic* with creating division within. Instead they tell mighty glamorous stories that anoint them as the most reputable elite warrior of that era. Leaving out the darkened secrets, how their mind-set combined thinking that is more alike with more negative rats and snakes, subplotting without true purpose, causing conflicting interest and conflicting agendas. Separation forms a rip in the group. Teams are segregated. The real versus the fake, a whole team breaks up into groups and factions of one whole, which used to be the strength. Compared like a female, so-called men run back in forth, gossiping like females involved in soap operas, creating conflict of mini wars of fistfights, which result in gunplay, team versus team after the initiated split. After defeating the enemy and him at a standstill, afraid to come within the war zone, enemy-inflicted victims are at the minimum, resulting in self-inflicted activities, becoming so dangerous that casualties of war within results in death. And the final chest moves, which sets the entire group apart. Either you take one side or the other within your family tribe, or you don't take any side because bad blood has already been spilled in the soil. The distrust, bad few seeds of apples, lack of loyalty, bragging rights of sleeping with an allies woman, touching your allies forbidden property. Disrespectful premonition of division causes the breakdown of unity and communications. A team falls apart. Agents within planted without knowledge. We had been betrayed from the beginning, not pinpointing our Jake the Snakes and true rats that were eating us alive inside, thus realizing that because you grew up together bonds can grow far apart. Women can be a vital reason adding to the demise of a group, as well as selfishness and sentimental values, with big egotistical individuals, unwilling to listen to reason. They affect the entire group. Not enough Indians and too many chiefs without structure and order designed a group that will not stand; but order and stipulations mandated have to be immaculately superb, not outstanding and demoralizing request of code of honor, simple and easy to carry out. The more complicated, the more rules will be dishonored. Men have become teams but have fallen because when power is obtained, men get greedy and change, becoming tyrants and dictators, forcing their own sentimental agendas to sustain themselves and quench their own thirst to rule with the thumb.

Upon gaining freedom after being released, emancipated, liberated from "the underground, underworld of prison," men who have become renowned men, rehabilitated in mind and body and soul, are back on the block, back to the hood. They returned, enticed by the allure of shining things. In prison, time is almost in pause mode, standstill, except for the gang violence and conduct. It's so easy to end up back in the system with a new jail term sentence, and that it is easier to reenter the criminal outlaw, crime-addicted elemental street progressiveness.

He is declined and rejected of employment because of the appearances of oneself and a racial profile that simply denies you equal opportunity. He is unable to provide or support anyone of dependency, who may happen to rely on your gain of livelihood and sufficient income distribution to help support one's family. Men are put up against the gun in between a rock and a hard place. Some revert back into the life of crime. It is much easier to permit oneself to be able to provide a meal for supper. It is much harder to be labeled as an ex-felon and told not to lie on an application, to be honest, as an honest civilian, time and time again. Months turn into years, while you remain honest. Applications mount up, with no return. Phone calls are attempted to assist a man rehabilitated and determined to succeed and follow the correct path, to do what is right! On the other hand, if this not the righteous side of man-made law of infractions and contradiction, the allure is enticing to a struggling man, up against the odds. Society is always giving men of this valor an old-fashioned beat down, only to believe maybe he is suffering for something he had done so many years ago. But in his own irony, he knows that his mistakes are not worth the cost of losing his family, enduring such poverty.

It becomes easier for a man to revert back, picking up that old rusty .45 or that sack of drugs and reposting himself out on the block, accumulating more in a few days than he have accumulated after being released for over two years. No matter what the results may be, if a man has tried with all efforts against him to live honestly, some men will indulge themselves into crime just to support their families. Every man endures a situation differently. When they are so confused and struggling, the only way they can find a simple solution to is to go back to the old way. He will undergo any drastic measurements in order to protect or support his family, even if it means that death is imminent, even if he has to stand on the block with dread in his heart, resenting to do wrong in the ghetto, submerged deep within a war zone of the hood and gang-active affiliates, armed and dangerously protecting his own means of survival.

The Notorious Compton Avenue
Crips Watts Darkside D. Blocc 95.7un str
Rest in peace Loool Ant3 Jaycee Ant1 T.Zone Dee Dee
Ric Dog1 Zeike Lucky Insane Duccy

The Cadilac which was in the Menace 2 Society
Scene Compton Avenue
As the white guy approaches the Actor whom say's hope you find your way down

"The Tired Poor Man who Had to Commit Wrong to Keep his Family Fed" (poetry)

How alluring are the big fancy shining cars, the fast life of automobiles and big guns, Harley Davidson, beautiful women as fly as movie stars, money, and gals at a fast pace like driving a car and never ending the race. The faster you drive, the faster you crash, in pursuit of the almighty dollar, a chase for the cash, because a slow life isn't fast enough, when you are not quick enough, in hot pursuit, tires squealing and pealing and turning the hard pavement into smokescreens of dust. Either you're quick or fast. You avoid the long arm of the law and the swift handcuffs. You hang with the boys mesmerized by the glamor of their toys, enduring a life of perplexity, seeking to be employed with all hope that you continue to resist the ill fate of temptations of joys. Until you became fed up, despite the complexity, you continued to keep your head up. You drove slow in your lane while you maintained focus. You decided you had enough, then you sped up, tires squealing and rubber burning and smoking. The systematic society mistakes a man as a boy. Every job interview ends with a void. Until this man decided to get dirty and not take this bullshit no more. Now the money is revealing, very appealing, stacked so high it poured out the windows and broke through the ceilings. My life as a criminal is paying off. No one would listen until I reverted back to being a villain. Now my jokes aren't funny, but I receive all the attention. And yes, I can retire before I receive a pension. Poor man talks. No one hears him. I'm rich, and everybody listens. Money rules everything around me. Life was cruel and unusual until money found me. The masses laughed and looked at me like a clown with dignity. In return, I smiled, but in reality, it was a smile turned upside-down! I needed all the help in the world, but even an ant will kick a dinosaur when he is on the ground. Diligently, I would dust off my knees, take a breath of the winter fresh breeze, pull up my bootstraps, and lift myself up off the ground. The day would come when I shall be number one, and "Ain't no fun when the rabbit got the gun." Got to have it in your heart to never give up and always keep your head up. No matter how tired you get, just don't get fed up.

Rise of the Bloods and Crips (Gladiator School), All-In, All-Out Street Wars

Over the years, dating back as far as 1960 up until 2012, more blacks have died in the state of California than anywhere else in the United States! With the lack of employment, word travels how difficult it is to obtain a job from state to state. The only tourist attracted to the state of California now is the criminal-minded and crop growers. "Most black men have relocated into prison or the cemetery."

Those who have survived the wars of the late 1970s up until now have moved out, formulating a new and improved black flight, in the same fashion as how blacks overtook the state of California and many other states and cities in the 1960s during the migration period. The white families packed their things and took flight. Thus, the beginning of white flight was initiated. With the flooding of California because of the Mexican borders residing so close to California, it has become overrun, overpopulated with Hispanic. Per ratio, there are approximately eight Mexicans to every two blacks: Crips versus Crips during the mid-1980s. No one understood how you could represent Crips and be at war with each other, not understanding how you could be a black man in general and commit black-on-black crime. Crips have different factions or tribes. For example, if you grew up in a state, and you and the children you grew up with formed a crew, and you were raised in the area and protected the people in the area, who were all close relatives and family members, of some sort related; but because of the era of the time, crews came around in your terrain, testing your group or crew's skills, intending to take, beat, violate, disrespect, everyone in your neighborhood, claiming it and the area as their own compared with a king and his castle, protecting his throne, preventing any foreigners or violators with plans of evil intent to conquer the turf, taking the throne with brute force, claiming it for themselves. So in order to maintain or remain respected, avoiding being violated, you had to protect your grounds that you grew up representing those streets as king and loyal soldiers of the tribe! For the cause was once to battle the infamous spook hunters, but since there was not many of them around anymore because of white flight, now the battles were against rival clicks or crews because you had no one else to battle against. Kids wanted to be notarized as the biggest, toughest, well-respected, baddest crews. When you came around, cats bowed their heads and rolled out the purple carpet because your crew was a force to be reckoned with. All the girls wanted a piece of the fellows, and all the younger guys wanted to be the fellows, and everyone else wanted to take the spotlight and the glory so they would have all the shine and glory that came along with it. To be the best, you had to beat the best in the battle zones. The Crips were known for bringing large numbers and being like the pirates of the Caribbean or the Vikings, menacing and rude. They were the raiders of the city and not the sea. Every place they traveled, they abduct that turf and place members of the Crips around, proclaiming its newest territories. This was the advanced kids' game, the newest fad of conquering turfs. And every day they would ask you what set you are from, until you grew tired of the beatings and submitted, announcing that you are Crips till death. The punishment stopped, and you were greeted as the newest member. The dictator of that sector would be appointed as the Crips shot callers. The Crips all decided what they would call their newest conquered neighborhoods, a slogan that would stick the appointed hood or gang identification, which describes what click of the Crips you were from. Those gang terms would last more than half a century. Whoever knew that something that started so small would grow worldwide, spreading throughout the continents. Some groups weren't strong enough and gave their thrones up without even throwing a punch, submitting and surrendering their flags and converting, so their king or shot caller became the soldier who followed someone else's dictatorship. Along with his crew, they were also re inverted and forced to become a faction of the mighty Crips or else suffer the pain and punishment every day until you submit. Meetings were appionted and subjects would be discussed about certain individuals or groups who held out, refusing to convert. A bone-crushing crew would be ordered to pay that group a visit every day until they had chosen, making their last and final determination to become a certified Cripster and part of the alliance. With every group around them transforming, they had no other choice but to join, surrendering their flags to the powerhouse on the rise. After the takeover was complete, and majority of the city was completely transformed, and there were no other groups to conquer, the Crips would have gladiator schools in order to sharpen their tools and become elite thugs with magnificent fighting skills that was superb. So they would meet at secluded locations, sometimes with or without boxing gloves. Even the timid and very afraid kids developed some semiacceptable boxing skills that would sustain them in a confrontation. Scheduled meetings occurred. Discussions arose about grudge matches going back to set an example of some group that fought long and fairly well against the Crips before announcing their alignment with the Crips. Because this group fought harder, inflicting the same amounts of damage, it was decided that they wanted to go back with even bigger, badder, tougher Crips and see how this group would fair off in protecting their turf as the newest Crips factions. The strongest Crips factions would go through this process to defend their turf against other Crips sets. During the beginning, it was only meant as a training procedure in order to get everyone prepared for any sort of invasion or subplot of any future rival enemies until they were decided gangster or thug enough, climbing the charts of notoriety, gaining stripes upon indulging in all sorts of criminal acts while maintaining secrecy. Don't get caught announcing your commitment and loyalty, not telling one soul. Only the neighborhood knew about the deepest, most forbidden crimes; and if anyone else knew, it violated all pretense of the gang's conjunctions. And sometimes detrimental acts occurred to set forth an example, creating a strong wall, separating the weak from the strong, eliminating guys out of the equation, who were prone to having loose lips like females telling men's business, running their mouths wide open like a blow horn, knowing and spilling the beans about other people's private business in a very inadequate fashion just for gossip and the sake to snitch once the individual encountered any situation that caused him to face prosecution. Cats like this were found, and they didn't last long. Either you were with it, or you weren't. There was a punishment for snitching during the olden days, a high price called death, so no one wanted to face such high stakes. So even people who were just regular citizens learned to keep their mouths shut. Snitching became nonexistence. People could do things in broad daylight, and no one had seen or said a thing. The power the Crips had was extraordinary. They basically took the City of Angels by storm and surprise. A pure out effort of overtaking the entire city became the next agenda after realizing how great and fast the Crips had transformed every other gang. With the observance of other older gangs that came before the Crips, the older members sit and watched, learning all its genius methods but taking it to a totally whole new level. As a powerhouse on the rise, other groups joined at ease like a vacuum. The Crips was the biggest, baddest tidal wave on the block, the newest powerhouse.

They would practice daily with mini boxing matches, with fist to determine who held the elite hands and boxing skills. Many kids got battered and bruised, knocked out; but the next day, they were at it again, sometimes resulting in black eyes or missing teeth. The 1990s were evident of such events being a part of the American California history, looking in the face of many Triple O/gees, their teeth missing. Many of the older cats were gladiators; and a telltale sign existed when they would smile with pride and dignity and much confidence, for they knew they were wearing a badge of honor for the days of the infamous battle zone, setting apart the true men from boys. Either you would fight, or you would be forced until you got better and better, learning to keep and protecting your manhood from being taken because in prison, the cost of not knowing how to use self-defense during the early 1960s resulted in a cruel game of take or keep. Guys who could fight kept what was already theirs, and those guys who chose not to fight usually ended up being in a bad situation until they either learned or fought effusively, giving themselves a fighting chance.

Many of the Crips could have been professional boxers of some sort. Some of these guys were just actually that good with their hands, knocking someone out every time they threw a punch with an infamous one-hitter quitter. So many guys could have battled and trained, obtaining the golden gloves in the state of California alone. So much raw uncut talent is wasted because more guys saw it more fitting to become a Crips. To them, Cripping was much more rewarding, to roll with the biggest, baddest crew, being accepted and treated like ghetto superstars, a figment of our own creation. Being black, we are innovative. We can turn an idea into a reality, and the world will imitate and follow our lead. This is a fact. Playing drums, music, and dancing are all fields that we excel in. It's just culture and natural. Some people have to take two-year classes. A black child comes out of the wound dancing. Some are gifted with singing. But truth is we excel at most anything we truly put our minds to. With focus and concentration, we become elite and the best that has ever done it, even to the point of over exceeding. With the tactical brute force applied, many teens are physically beaten to a bloody pulp, neighborhood after neighborhood. And it's modest everyday civilians are being attacked, robbed, and rudely targeted, such as old men and old women. This Crips franchise was getting out of control and too big for their own bridges. They became all-out hoodlums, terrorizing their own environments, forgetting about how hard and how far we had come through, gaining rights through the Civil Rights movement, forgetting about how the Black Panther had taken a stand to help defend the people who were being assaulted by white hoards, a constant reminder of the violence against blacks. Yet the uprising immature Crips were too far along and too established with their mind-set. Those people who had something to say had waited until it was extremely so far ahead of itself that they obtained big egos and refuse to listen. After all, most of the older Panthers begin to get incarcerated, and the ones left behind were too tempted with the flood of drugs and profit. Either they used or they became big-time dealers. The lure of money and lots of it was too tempting. With that alone, the Crips noticed that some so-called good guys' hand are involved in the drug game. Some of the notarized peace marchers get their hands filthy. The Crips decided they wouldn't listen to anyone at all. No one would be able to dictate how they lived and dealt with situations.

The Bloods begin to gather secretively, accepting all the rejects or degenerates that the Crips refused or declined to allow representation of the flag. For some reason, they were considered rejects and not worthy to represent the four-letter word or the color blue. Meanwhile, so many young teens grew so tired of the Crips beating them up, taking their leather jackets and shoes, and even taking their lunch money. These young men begin to meet up in private areas, forbidding to be like the Crips and discussing on becoming brothers in arms, banding together to prevent this renegade tribe from coming through everyone's area or turf, and beating and bullying anyone and everyone who they felt were permitted to do such a thing to. It was outrageous. How dangerous and malicious they had become.

So many young teens are violated, beaten, battered, and bruised. They decided that this wouldn't go on anymore without some sort of retaliations in return, and the Bloods came to existence. With guys like T. Rodgers, O/gee Pudding, it was a finale. Bloods was the name, and Killing Crips would be their game.

The Bloods begin to increase in numbers because they were less violent, and the females thought their color of choice was pretty appealing. They initiated more females, but they also begin to pull in elite soldiers. Some Crips were known for stating that in some areas, the Bloods could've been Crips for how they conducted themselves, unruly and obnoxious, always ready to engage in wars; and if they were to put on blue, you would think that they were Crips. After all, the one thing we all inherited was the color brown, the skin of our race. We all wore it unproductively and without pride, which existed before the color blue and red; and we were all born humans and not gang affiliated or as slogans.

After the Crips began to notice the emergence of the Bloods and realizing that a few members were ex-Crips and one of their major factions in Compton had transformed, disowning the Crips totally, because of the constant camaraderie and bad blood after futile fights and lack of unity, tempers flaring, the Crips had begun to fight inwardly. So many different factions emerged all over the place. It seems as if everywhere, kids were representing Crips gangs, creating their own hood slogans without any say so or structure. The control was loosening with increasing numbers and newer subdivisions all over. Everyone was representing Crips, and the Piru's Crips in Compton disliked how the confusion was creating this renegade bully syndrome. Fight me for your respect, attitude, bigger-than-life egos. The Crips picked and chose fighting against other Crips to humiliate them in front of everyone, including the females. Because the older muscle bound, more fighting-prone Crips took pure advantage of the Crips that were less skilled in fighting, taking their women, beating them because they could. Some Crips went off and started their own Crips crews, and the other Crips turned Blood and with so much fueled animosity and anger. Because of the infamous gladiator schools, grudges were born. Some guys were angry because they had to fight some of the biggest bullies. These guys were huge. The Crips loved lifting weights, and it pays off to have a frontline of youth that are similar to lines men on a football team because of weightlifting. During the brief bouts of jumping into the ring of the battle zone, being pitted against someone standing six feet five inches, weighing 265 pounds—and your only five feet five inches tall and weighing 150 pounds—you hope for a miracle to save you. The Crips didn't hold back. They were known for beating other Crips like enemies during friendly boxing matches. Many Crips didn't like this part of the game, how the stronger, agile, experienced fighters would take advantage of their own crew members; and they were all the same. Big egos create the misled to become disgruntled. In private conversations, certain Crips begin to speak out against the inward abuse. Tempers flared. Grudges grew. The beatings were getting too vicious. When a Crips was knocked out, he would get stomped; and Crips are looking on, too afraid to speak out about the brutality. This was the fall of the empire that had just started. Grudges grew. Some guys never said a word. All the long climbing, the ranks, and once they became elite Bosses and had established their own Crips armies, the all-out Crips wars and old grudges were ignited. Because the simple mistake of one Crips' ego to pound another Crips Cuzzin to prove how monstrous you are, not realizing that your victim was just too young to win and too light to fight over abusing him. After many years on the prowl, climbing the charts in rank and jail sentence, he comes out with a faction of the Crips that he has established. He is muscular, with revenge on his mind and with blood being spilled because of his hands. He has become the monster you were when he faced you in the battle zone, seeking revenge. Scores are settled through a rematch, but tempers are uneasy as two different Crips sets watch as the two bosses tangle, toe to toe, squaring off, settling differences; but in the long run, differences aren't settled because of simple facts like these and minor altercations occurring over a long period of time. If two hoods go through mini fights and battles, with the younger generation inheriting a beef, they know nothing about. But they are born into a war over an old grudge for a long period of time, resulting in a few shootings and a couple of Crips being shot here and there. Once some Crips end up a murder statistic, this is how all-out, all-in wars between Crips were normally kicked off and begin. The infamous Crips-on-Crips wars, which mean when a life is lost, becomes catastrophic, a domino effect on both sides, losing life. War becomes imminent, and with death, you declare to inherit an enemy for life.

Amazing to say, an entire Piru's gang that was once Crips turned Bloods, giving them a gigantic increase and swell in numbers. If those events might not have occurred to this day, all Piru's in Compton would be Crips today. That is an amazing fact of history that never was. Being a Bloods in the 1980s meant unity. They called themselves United Blood Nation, all one and one together; but in the City of Angeles, they were outnumbered five to one. So they could not go anywhere without risking being assaulted by the Crips. So they were confined to remain within their own neighborhoods, almost like prisoners of the city. And once traveling out to shop, visit a girlfriend, or attend any important business, they usually would have to wear mutual colors to hide their affiliation with the Bloods. Discretion was the way of surviving while being of Bloods descent.

Too many Bloods were being brutally beaten. Once the Bloods were increasing in numbers, they had decided that they could seek revenge so they would schedule to combat the Crips at their own game of gladiators in the battle zones. Agreeing to meet at some secluded location and indulging in an all-out, fist-to-fist combat, the Bloods would arrive early, surveying the battlefields, placing weapons in secret hiding spots to help them even the scores. The Bloods had established faction. Just like the Crips, Bloods sets were all throughout various areas in Los Angeles. They had met and clashed in the battle zone many times before, but because of the large alarming numbers, the Crips were just too much for the Bloods. Nevertheless, their hearts were their biggest attributes. They were fearless, knowing they were going to be outnumbered. Even though they were outnumbered, they showed up ready and prepared to engage. They only wanted respect from the Crips. They demanded to be respected and be able to travel without any conflicts. The Crips felt differently. If they wanted respect, they would have to battle the Crips in the battle zone the same way each Crips had done it to achieve their own status quo of respect and stripes. Because the Crips were taught by the older gangs before their time, that respect was earned and not given. Gladiator school was the perfect way to settle scrimmages and grudge matches. It was organized and determined to use the school grounds in an attempt to subdue the violence and to keep the brute violence a dark kept secret within the school grounds with the large fences. It was difficult for guys who caught butterflies during the matches to run and flee. Everyone had to fight as warriors, and if you ran, you were subsequently captured and reaped even more brutal punishment for turning yellow bellied.

The Bloods always arrived early meeting at the secluded designated locations. The Crips allowed them to as much as they wanted because of their large overwhelming numbers, but the Bloods were just as active and brutal, with very strong hearts and courage. They would use tactics and plots of ingenuity to battle the Crips, sometimes hiding weapons in secluded spots near the points of engagement where the battle would occur. This unforeseen method would assist the Bloods that were severely outnumbered to increase their numbers. And even out the balance, they neutralize the Crips in a five to one ratio per in the battle zone. The Crips arrived at some other location and waited for a few hours, both gangs with numbers of participants increasing enormously by the seconds as they begin to plan their attack. The Crips appointed a group of scouts to go on a mission to retrieve vital Intel about the Bloods, a count of how many had arrived inside the gladiator school as well as names. Sizes were all advantages. Every detail was important to the Crips because the Bloods sit waiting for the Crips, but they normally show up late without any respect. The Bloods thought it was the reason. But that, of course, wasn't the reason. It was a designed trap to pay the Bloods back for all the battles. When they had pulled weapons and began to gain a better edge of the battle, the odds normally changed to their favor as Crips. That was considered a violation, so they would considered that the Crips had won those battles because they used fist, and most of the Bloods used weapons. The Crips decided they would not change the rules that had been implied, allowing the Bloods to brandish weapons, because they were outnumbered. Now that wasn't nearly the fact anymore, because the Bloods were increasing in numbers; and during this session, nearly 150 Bloods had arrived, meeting at the school grounds, ready to battle the Crips in the designated battle zone (Locke High). Located between Avalon and San Pedro, it was the perfect grounds set for engagement. Afterward, the Bloods could meet and gather at the nearest Bloods set located near the battle zone. The nearest Blood headquarters would be the infamous and notoriously known Bounty Hunter Bloods. The projects could secure them and doom any Crips seeking to enter with the many dead-end puzzles like a maze. The streets were death traps. It would be insane to enter that place known as the Nickerson Gardens Projects. The Crips had planned as their numbers swell to as many as 350 known Crips sets from the east side and west side Crips. They figured they would only send 175 soldiers into the battle zone to engage in the gladiators' preliminary matches. Their true intentions were to hurt as many as possible, and after they thought the battle was over or if some had attempted to run and flee, they would be captured while attempting to jump the fences. The Crips had set an elusive line all around the school. Some were inside the fence, and other Crips were outside the fence, waiting with weapons to hand to the Crips on the inside of the battle zone, who were engaged in an all-out, bone-crushing, nail-biting, face-smashing, foot-stomping, head-busting, old-school medieval gladiators' melee. If they needed any weapons, the Crips were simply ready to use them against the Bloods attempting to get away. The additional one hundred Crips yielding weapons surrounded the outside area of the gladiator school, while the remaining seventy-five Crips in covert slashed the tires of the Bloods vehicle that were not occupied, taking the cars that had keys and beating the pulp out of the Bloods who were just the getaway drivers. And carjacking them for their vehicles would cause other Bloods to suffer being stranded when the brawling was over, which they would have run through nearly two miles of Crips territory. Luckily, they had chosen the battle grounds that gave them an option to make it to the Nickerson's gardens plenty of battles before. Without thought, they were manipulated to agreeing to terms and meeting at locations where, if the battle was ended, there wasn't a safe zone for more than twenty-five miles on foot, because after brawls, people who walked in with you were nowhere in sight. And the Crips territory was massive. They would be out hunting for stragglers after brawls. Some of the Bloods who were the getaway drivers yielded and brandished revolvers. Upon pointing it at the Crips, the Crips ran off into the shadows of the late night and disappear, yelling, screaming out loud. They got guns, alarming other Crips of the danger they encountered. The Crips backed off, allowing the Bloods who had been severely beaten to grab some of their soldiers off the battlefield and take them back to their headquarters to let their female soldiers attend to their battle wounds.

Meanwhile, those Crips and Bloods who were comatose, unaware that the battle zone was flooded with what appeared to be limp, lifeless, bloody, broken-up young men's bodies lying everywhere. Some had fallen out in alleys, trying to escape, but their wounds were too severe so they were unable to get very far. Some were knocked out in the battle zone, with broken legs and arms, unable to run. Approximately thirty soldiers, more or less, lay in the battle zone. Those who were able to flee never returned, assuming they had killed someone. All the blood was spilled throughout the school grounds. If you were too hurt to be carried out, you had to crawl and scratch your way to a local hospital or someplace where you could receive medical attention. Weapons lay everywhere in the battle zone, bloody and broken from cracking skulls open. Even while injured with broken legs and arms, and with severe skull fractures, these crazed maniacs lay broken up; yet they seemed to be that angry, attempting to reach out and cause more pain upon an already fallen and disabled soldier. Hurting alike, two remaining warriors began to think of confronting each other, unable to escape and flee. Even the cripple and wounded crawled toward a broken and bloody weapon nearby. Coherent, some were still able to engage in a handicapped match of fairly injured and almost out for the count. One Bloods and one Crips made it to their feet and began to swing weapons at each other in slow motion, missing the mark, missing the target. They were barely breathing, looking at each other, weapons in hand. They both crashed and fell back to the ground. The mighty blows they had unleashed upon each other took its toll. All the energy they had remaining had been exalted during the handicap mismatch. They were lying flat on their backs, gazing up at the heavens, breathing extremely hard, almost gasping for one final breath. Each of the two remaining Crips and Bloods engaged in this crippling last man standing game, or shall I say last men out on the ground, counting the stars, looking effusively up as the dark skies light up by the shining bright stars; and the moon cycle was full. With blood dripping from their skulls, bones snapped in half, some victims lie with bones protruding from their clothing. The two coherent Crips and Bloods attempted to finish each other off after realizing they were all alone. With nearly thirty Bloods and Crips hurt so severely, they were unable to be carried off. Their wounds were too severe to carry themselves off the battlefield, with all that was left in their nearly lifeless bodies. They could only look at each other and at all the almost lifeless corpses that lay beaten so badly. Some were in comas. With no one around or with not a sound of life coming from the bodies on the ground lying all over the place, the two coherent but severely damaged enemies, Blood and Crips, devised and communicated that if they didn't come together to assist each other, they were all going to be discovered the next day, deceased; and no one would ever piece together what had happened. Either they would join forces and become brief allies for the moment and attempt to find some sort of help. They both talked, asking one another what Bloods set and Crips sets they were from and announcing what their names were, after their acquaintances that seem to be all but strange. Knowing who and where each other's stomping grounds were located, a team could be dispatched to come out and reap havoc upon the other, despite the vital Intel. It was that much more detrimental to help one another. After all, both of their comrades, their team of soldiers, have departed; and the rules always remain the same. If you're too hurt or become a statistic, you will not get carried or pick up off of the battlefield unless you can pick up yourself. No one wants to be implicated in some sort of crime, if you are somewhere close to death or even an actual victim resulting to being beaten so severely that you succumb and die to your wounds. No one wants to carry a soldier that is nearly beaten to death, and they are the ones accused of the murder because they are the last ones seen with the victims. So during and before engagement, the rules are stated. Afterward, any many unable to be removed is responsible for himself. Every man is accountable for his own livelihood. Knowing the rules and factors, they both reach out, grabbing old, broken, and bloody 4x4 and converting them into semi crutches. Then they both leaned on each other to assist the other's dead weight. And leaning on the bloody 4x4, they both stood erect and hold each other up. The Crips had a broken leg and a fractured arm. The Bloods had a broken arm and a sprung ankle, but they were able to rely on each other as one in order to seek more sufficient and effective help. They had no other choices left to determine but to help themselves. They both joked. The Crips said with a sense of humor, "Man, that bright ass red you're wearing is killing me. I can barely see cuzz you so damn flamed up its blinding me." He was squeezing his eyes to display that his eyes were being damaged. The Bloods returned, "I'm so battered and bruised like the rest of these fools that look dead I should have been a Crips." In dismay, the Crips responded, "What the hell's that suppose to mean, man?" The Blood replied, "Forget about it, man. It's nothing. I was just trying to come back with my own joke, but my pain got my mind so damn cloudy I can't even think." The Crips responded as they were taking small steps forward, "I can feel you on that, Cuzz!" The Bloods looked at the Crips in disbelief. Being called a Cuzz was an insult. The Crips said, "Man, I forgot." The Bloods responded, "Bloods, It's all right." Now the Crips looked confused. He had never been called Bloods by an actual Bloods member. They both laughed at each other while hopping along in severe disgruntling pain. Saying to one another, "Man, you remind me of my family." They both agreed. "Man, we just might be related. It's a small world. You never know," the Bloods had said out loud. "If we make it, man, if I come and look you up, will your home boys trip?" the Bloods asked. "Because the Crips are acting crazy, we are starting to fight each other. We got too many factions, and it's getting stupid being a Crips. Ain't like it was at the beginning, a few years ago when we had first begun. It's too much jealousy nowadays." The Bloods responded, "Don't be fooled. We're getting much larger, but more Bloods are acting like Crips. I sometimes think they want to be Crips because we fight too. It's kept quiet. After all, there too many Crips for us to be fighting." The Crips laughed, saying, "Yeah. But you, dudes, are real sneaky and sly. I give that too you." They finally got near the front gate exit, and they had gathered themselves because they both were going to be heading off into two different separate locations. And the next time they would meet, they didn't know if it would be as friend or foe. The two injured soldiers limped off into the night, one going right and the other going left. Stating, "I'll catch you later." The Bloods replied, "I'll catch you later, Dog." Neither one looked back, and they went on their way, living another day to tell a story alike many others. In comparison, that would be a part of the California history, the lifestyle, and the antics of the Crips and Bloods who could determine whether the next time these guys would meet, time changing a decade later, the shootings and highest murder rates begin. Because some guys couldn't take the beatings and grueling unfair punishment that the battle zone issued out, a new increased war tactic was born.

The Billy the Kids and gunslingers replaced the Muhammad Alis and Joe Fraziers. Fighting was the way to be killed, and shooting became the way to be king of the hill. It was as cowardly as you can think, but when a man kills a fighter and the fighter versus the gunslinger, the gun proved victorious every time. Even the fighters begin packing to defend themselves. The late 1970s were fading out, and the Crips and Bloods begin to forget about the long black jackets that the Black Panthers had worn, materializing as an iconic statement of fashion and representing power, which meant to initiate strength with the color black; even though we are brown-skinned people. The 1980s came in with a pistol blaze of glory. The style of the Crips was very different, but because of watching old gangster movies with Al Capone, Bugsy Siegel, Machine Gun Kelly, Bonnie and Clyde, the Crips idolized how they dressed and dealt with the society; so they attempted to imitate their styles but with a different twist. The Crips sported ace deuces, Crock-a-sacks, Stacy Adams, godfather hats, suspenders, canes. And a blue bandanna was the fashion statement that indicated that you were a notarized Crips. With co-founding elite Crips-in-charge Raymond Washington, Stanley (Tookie) Williams, pushed the lines from the east to the west. Big Tookie was an intimidating figure known for body building and lifting everything he could touch. He became the epitome of what a Crips should look like during battle zone. Gladiator school young men feared these two co-founders. Raymond Washington was known as a vicious, intimidating fighter, raised up on the east side. And Stanley Williams was just as vicious but more intimidating than any one had ever imagined. He looked like the Incredible Hulk with brown skin. With these two at the realms, being a Crips was a must because their names had become street legend. August 9, 1979, Raymond Washington was subsequently gunned down and murdered at the age of twenty-five years. Raymond Washington disagreed with the use of weapons because he grew up fighting. He was also known as a short-tempered bully. Very few people liked him. He was well respected by those who were just like him. The Crips personified and took on all the traits of Stanley (Tookie) Williams and Raymond Washington's brutal, obscene, derogatory attitudes of "me against the world." Everyone grew up emulating all that they had done. Many Crips were being trained on how to get their Cripping on, a quote derived by many futuristic

Crips to indicate that they were down for all causes, riding out, putting in work on enemies and civilians alike in order to obtain financial profit and mostly to achieve street creditability to add to that notoriety hyphened next to your name. Whenever it was mentioned in the categories of street legends, each Crips strive to surpass every other Crips, gaining stripes and respect. So by the time Raymond Washington was murdered and Stanley (Tookie) Williams was arrested for three counts of murder, the Crips who were raised up under their wings had risen to the occasion of street notoriety. They begin winging and teaching the next generation of renegade Crips. The rise and spread was complete. Now the wars were brewing and imminent to become fatal in the ghettos. The '80s crime rate had increased, especially murder, and the black people were suffering at the forefront of the brute violence. The big bad bully syndrome the Crips had adopted from their two immature young leaders had become the all-Crips anthem. They lived by this motto and victimized their own people by these senseless immoral acts. While in prison, Raymond Washington received word through fellow inmates, who were affiliates of the Black Guerrilla family, an old original prison gang that combated White Supremacist Aryan Brothers and the Mexican gangs. They approached Raymond, discussing how his street gangs, young and without structure, were killing so many blacks. Some members of the Guerrilla family were affected by the crimes committed by the Crips because their own family was murdered by senseless crimes the Crips had carried out. The Guerrilla family wanted to kill Raymond Washington. After all, he was the first and only Crips in prison. He was given a pass, receiving knowledge in prison. He began to think about his creation. The black Muslims began to educate him during his youth. He could barely read or write. This was part of the reason he liked to fight kids who teased. While in prison, he was tutored about black history, and he began to realize the biggest crime against his people. And he was helping carry it out, being young without vision, starting a gang in secret. He couldn't see through the smokescreens, what the Panthers had been doing, but after the conspiracy to remove them now in prison, the picture was painted much clearer: how all the other gangs popped up from all over after the demise of the Panthers. They kept the streets clean. He never knew that the Crips would become the most powerful gang in the city, with alarming numbers that have never been seen before. The Guerrilla family members were political prisoners, created in the same pretense of the Panthers, but more ruthless and seeking to add to their power structure in numbers. Some had been incarcerated for nearly fifteen years, educating themselves, becoming thinkers. They knew if they were able to convince Raymond Washington with all young and criminal minded Crips, it was just a matter of time before they were receiving life sentences and be sent to prison to encounter the Guerrilla family. So if somehow they could spread word to Raymond Washington to form some sort of alliances or maybe even convert the Crips to become part of the Guerrilla family upon entering prison, they would be successful. But first of all, they would have to gain success with influencing Raymond while he served his sentence in prison. They achieved educating Raymond, but he determined that he would remain a Crips. His purpose was to end the new arising gun play that had escalated Crips versus Crips versus Bloods. The Crips were out of control, and with Raymond being the creator, he figured he could change the inward fighting. And with so many splinter cells of Crips everywhere you looked or traveled, jealousy began to spread. The Crips were the most violent and had accomplished adding to the amount of stripes and work put in during Cripping and terrorizing the entire City of Angeles. Crips hood went to war just to prove who could commit the most murders and drive bys, inflicting the most casualties. Shootings became common. Thanks to the televisions, the Crips are now adding the infamous drive-bys of the 1920s to their reckless image and portfolio, their newest bag of tricks. Raymond Washington had no clue what he was going to encounter once he was released from prison. The image of the Crips grew bigger than he could ever imagine. When he started, it was just him in the beginning, with a handful of young men. He hung out with shooting marbles and mimicking the older guys that were in charge of the streets during his very young years. Many years later, gang numbers tripled with affiliates well within the thousands. He knew that it would be very difficult trying to convince young men with guns to stop shooting. Applying brute force was a thing of the past. It could get you killed, so he couldn't approach them with the disciplinary act. After all, it was the reason so many Crips began picking up guns. In the first place, it seems to be as if he was left with no other choice. If he couldn't control or reach the army he had started, he would denounce them and step away from the onslaught of violence and pray that his creation didn't mistake his newfound righteous values and emancipated thinking, releasing the shackles of the mind as a sign of weakness and considering-him a target as well. He was a change man, a free man. His agenda's were different. His mind had broken free from the invisible shackles. He only anticipated to do the same thing with the gang he had created, releasing them from their own prison that barricaded their success. Back to the streets, hanging with the boys, quietly paying attention, he noticed how much things had changed and so many Crips had been recruited. He didn't know who was who, and it was out of control. They idolized him, but the envy was imminent because Crips on the rise had obtained crews, and they controlled their own blocks and Crips sets. They were the boss, and with Raymond Washington out, they feared he would do the same that Tookie Williams had had done when he was out, focusing the spotlight and stealing the shine from the leaders of different sectors. Well respected and as the innovators, it was easily conceived that you would become subjugated to losing your status quo position of rank to the two well-respected colossus figures of men whose reputation had well proceeded them in the gang life. There was no honor among thieves. While some Crips were not excellent fighters, they were even better shooters, knowing if a greater-than-life figure stood before them, it was either kill or be killed. They also possessed skills of uncanny suggestions and intellectually inclined in deception to conquer at all means necessary. With gaining power, men become greedy and sentimental, envious of the next man that has acquired the almost kinglike status. Rivalries were established. Whenever Tookie Williams came around, it was like as if a movie star like Clark Gabriel had pulled up. Many Crips revered and feared him and his hulking figure. When you're on top, people's intentions are not always moral. Your own friends shall attempt to help you become unstable and weak-minded so that they can keep your thinking process off balanced, providing you with drugs and alcoholic beverages, while conspiracies are orchestrated. But with Tookie Williams, he became more like all the renegades of Crips; and with full-time engagement in the warfare, you become well and highly negotiable as a true rider, diminishing any notions of being overthrown because of the repercussion that may be initiated. Tookie Williams knew that he was an opposing figure, and he also knew that the envy was strong, and that many up-and-coming Crips wanted to take his throne. So he played chess, aligning himself with the original imposing figures as equals and winging young soldiers and keeping them surrounding him to watch his back wherever he traveled. And when in other Crips hoods, he made sure he knew the top ranked soldiers and leaders that would accompany him throughout his visit. Every hood he went to, he was like a celebrity and was well protected because he treated people as family. Once in a while, unleashing that Crips deity to allow other Crips to overstand, I am with the business. Also, this became a method used to keep the younger, more challenging Crips distant. Sometimes this meant being dysfunctional and extra violent knocking someone out, so that all the others could visualize the exquisite punching power and refuse to ever challenge you in a duel of fist fighting or to never question your authority the same way a father disciplines his son. Tookie knew these things; that's why he became torn with doing right and wrong. You begin to want to change to help your people; but of all the street elements, the fame and glory of indulging in inflicting and teaching lessons to adversaries, attempting to violate your pride and defending it can create you into becoming a monster who loves and craves the feeling of destroying any opposing force, seeking to end. You are making it that much easier to hurt and maimed individuals. Raymond Washington was released from prison, and with his newfound knowledge, he began discussing a change that didn't sit well with other Crips. He could sense the change of guard and the resentment toward his opinions of a one-umbrella ruled empire of Crips. With one boss, this form of dictatorship was refused by many leaders of the many Crips factions, to give that power up to be ruled by one king. No Crips was going to allow that to happen. After all, most of the new Crips only heard of the legend and hadn't seen him. Plus they were in the Crips killing business as well, so they who were the most ranked had the most to lose if Raymond Washington had decided to form one Crips umbrella united. So unfortunately Raymond was killed, shot down on the corner of Sixty-Fourth and

San Pedro after walking up to a vehicle, which was against his rules and standards. He would never do such a thing, as quoted by everyone who knew him. Obviously, he knew the killer, and rumor says that the closest one to you will do you. At the time, he was more likely closer to Crips, but that is just an assumption. No one knows the truth, but the people involved in the shooting and that person, of course, Raymond Washington; but dead men have no tale to tell, but every once in a while, they can speak from the grave and paint a more exclusive and vivid picture of the details involved in their undetermined demise. The men involved are probably not even on this terrain anymore. Who knows? Maybe if Raymond could've lived, maybe we would have witnessed a change and a decrease of some of the lost lives because he was actually trying to form a peace treaty with the Bloods. And I'm quite sure many Crips didn't want that after all the deaths that occurred to their hands. Anything may have transpired. Old wounds are hard to heal, and dating back to the days of gladiator school, vengeance remained in the heart of so many of the brutally pummeled victims who had suffered embarrassment because of his lethal hands. After all, Raymond Washington was known as a bully in his youth, establishing many who disliked him. With the emergence of guns, the weakest link stood as the strongest man alive. I can imagine a coward fighting and losing so much, he purchased a gun and with possession of a small arms such as a .22 revolver. That person became the most feared man to be reckoned with, after pulling the gun, firing in the air or maybe shooting into the crowd, noticing how the crowd disbursed and scattered, running, fearing for their lives. They risked being shot down in the streets. He recognized that even the biggest and baddest man alive couldn't beat or defeat the gun, so he initiated the gun as his Excalibur sword and swore to keep it by his side as his equalizer, paving the way for many generations to come: small, tall, fat, skinny, and mentally challenge would use the weapon of choice for protection against the world of gangs who became dependent and reliable on the gun. The power manifested after revealing the gun, that which makes grown men shake and shiver and shrink while living in their own skin, the power that a boy gains after knowing he possesses the tool that makes him equal to all men who disagrees. The magnitude of many lengths the boy will take to receive the juice, to gain stripes, adding shields upon his sleeves or shoulders. This monster was created, thanks to all the many elements, all the battles, and all handicap matches when smaller guys fought guys in the battle zone, unfairly forced and pummeled. They had no chance against all these. Elements were factors to the attributes and emergence of the firearms. After all, so many other weapons were being used that resulted in the loss of lives. Someone just had decided why not equal the disadvantages? If an old lady is mugged time and time again, and she purchases a .44 magnum, then she becomes evenly advantaged and strongly protected the next time a mugging occurs, only if she brings forth her large Excalibur to present it as the modernized peacemaker of justice. And she'll say, "Let me alone or eat the lead, suckers." I guarantee that the so-called muggers will end up running and telling a tale about an old lady who didn't play around.

In 1980, the murder rate in Los Angeles skyrocketed. What is ironic is that the previous year before, Raymond Washington was murdered. The murder rate increased drastically for two years in a row after his death. If the gangs' retaliation methods were just as identical to the way gangs normally send out crews to reap retribution of today's time, I could only imagine with facts and comparison and mere incidence that occurred because of the death that increased the murder rate compared with the five years before Raymond Washington's murder! Even though it was mentioned that Crips were all but responsible, I take it with the lack of leadership and irrational impulsive thinkers ready to explode and seek revenge against the Bloods for pass crimes, the Raymond Washington murder was the excuse used to tip the iceberg: 1975—556 murders, 1976—517 murders, 1977—574 murders, 1978—678 murders, 1979—817 murders, 1980—1028 murders. In the year that Washington was killed, notice during the years before how steady and common the murder rate differential was. And in 1979, the same year Washington was shot and killed, nearly two hundred extra murders were committed. In 1980, the year after his death, what had happened the year before spilled over into the beginning of the 1980s, creating the new innovative killer Capitol elite and murder rates that would spiral upward for many more decades, spreading throughout all the states in America, setting the trends for a new and improved, advanced game of seek and destroy gang warfare. This well-kept secret was isolated until crack hit the city and gang members begin to travel, taking with them the way of the Crips and Bloods. The gang bang or die mentality and the exploitation of the movie *Colors* showed the world how to become an effective Blood and Crips; and with the exploitation of scare face, it showed the Crips and Bloods how to get money and become politically inclined, changing their appearances, and how to become productive businessmen and gangsters, all at once increasing their revenue. The main interior motives and goals are money, power, and respect. The scare face mimicking took effect all over in various cities. Every street hustler wanted to become bigger than his competitors. With gangs involved, you enhance their aspects of activities. What they love doing is the way they will live and the product in which they would invest their monies in war. Compare the rates of murder before the emergence of crack! Rap music with its monotone alluring us into a musical trance a dreamlike state, the word play and lyrical slang, we go all out to imitate the profound words of lyrical technique, which was derived back in the early '60s and '70s, the days of the Mack and Super fly. The pimps were the iconic figurers who kids simply wanted to be. They were cool, and they were the ones driving the big fancy car, and they had all of the money and women, and they were respected in the streets by the streets. When rap emerged, it took the riddle and rhyming of the Mack and Pimp, combining it with coolness and modernized time, thus creating rap. Notice how every decade, as time evolves with technology, so does terminology and street slang and the street characters. In the 1960s, you had the Black Panthers. Jazz was fading, and rock and roll and soul were emerging. Black-and-white televisions began to evolve into colored televisions. The unity of the Civil Rights movement was in full effect. And being black and proud was the way. The 1970s saw the rise of the Pimps Glamor. Although the Pimp had been around, in the 1970s, his image was forefront in Hollywood eyes, making him an iconic figure. Street hustlers begin to hit the scene, scamming, coning, plotting for a come up, a quick hustle for a few bucks. R&B soul was replacing soul music. The love songs were changing to a faster pace, "disco music." The Afro replaced the slick back perms, and women wore more fitting-type clothing, throwing the old dresses of concealment of the '60s into the garbage and began showing the world their big waistlines and brick-house bodies, with bell bottoms advertising the black women's huge bottoms that had been hidden with the large dresses but inherited in many generations. The 1980s was the emergence of the gang. The fall of the Black Panthers that transpired in the mid-70s resulted in the gathering of rising hustling and scamming crews. In the 1980s, with the void of the Panthers, these crews became gangs, fighting and claiming turfs in the same fashion as Great Britain claiming America as its own; and wars broke out with the American Indians and the Spaniards, and America was fighting for liberty. The gangs wanted to claim territories since the Panthers were not around to enforce the law like they had done many years before forcing groups to go inside and keep their filth under the carpet and out of the public view of our children. The dealer was the newest kid on the block, and he rolled with the gangs so he supplied his members with support and the knowledge on how to make money dealing the new innovative crack street pharmaceutical. Rap music was on the move along with break dancing and graffiti writing on walls. The dress code changed every decade along with the music and elements of the streets. More jumpsuits were the style because they were considered loose, and with a lifestyle of ducking and dodging the law, it was more adequate for escaping a cop in hot pursuit. The Gerri Curls were in. Gang violence increased drastically in some parts of the United States. In the 1990s, the flattops of Kid n Play, the new and improved hairstyle of the eraser heads, were in. The infamous LA Rodney King Riots and the short-term peace treaty between the Crips and Bloods stemmed the violence to a ceasefire. Rap music stormed in at the forefront. Conflicting it was the new innovative gangster rap music. Explicit with its views, it caused much controversy. Spilling into the streets, the gangs had spread, especially the gangs from the state of California. The Bloods and Crips were almost in every state in America. Rap music was paving the way to its identity called hip-hop. Crack allowed poor families to discover what traveling and skiing meant. After all, the black families have only seen what the life outside the ghetto looked like through watching televisions, but now with crack, any black kid could make it big. And many attempted; thus, crack began to flood the states along with the gangs, providing a way out of the ghetto. All these elements combine as a match made, creating America's own nightmare, the menace of society, the serial killers of the hoods. Now rap music associated with gang life; and it associated with crack epidemic, which resulted in quick money, fast cars, beautiful women, shining jewelry, style with clothing, and glamor in an imaginable life and being from some sort of gang, allowing you to venture and become secured with hood fellows, and providing the means to activate soldiers at your dispense. With connection and street creditability, you could spread the wealth. Rappers usually lived the street life, transforming it to a less gruesome term for rappers on the way out of the hood. Accustomed to the profile of the streets, they created hip-hop during the 1980s till the 1990s Most rappers knew of people involved in the street life, so they were able to give vivid details about the life, painting the picture in their songs. Some political rappers sprinkled their songs with a deep and provocative message. After the 1980s and 1990s, rap lost the message in the music that created the term, "Hip-hop is dead with no rules or street codes, all the same elements." Controversial gangster music was all vital to the comprehension expanse of the ill-rational thinkers because they would take the music and use it as aspiration to inflict crime because of their lack of concern and maturity, misusing the true purpose of warnings before destruction, because the world discovered that sex and violence do sell and well. Being a rap artist, they had to lure you in with violence then after gaining notoriety sneak wisdom and street knowledge into the music to get you to second-think your attributes to the increased murder rates and involvement of the gang life. The year 2000, the year of Y2K, the change of the millennium, cell phones are the biggest fad, erasing the use of ground lines. In the early '80s, only street hustlers carried cell phones, and it meant you were well connected in the streets. In the year 2000, everyone and their mother had a cell phone, and every black man and women wanted the world to know they were important. So much spilled conversation hit the streets, it became an epidemic. Gossip was at an all-time high. All you had to do was stand a block away, and as loud as black people whisper, you would be able to tell the world about their all-but-not-anymore-private life. Some people talk so loud! And they have the nerve to say, "Why are you listening so hard to my private conversation?" With the cell phone on broadcast worldwide, with loud horn speaker phone, the privacy factor is already nonexistent. The truest loyal street code had died out with the three-strike law put in effect in numerous states. In Los Angeles, it became effectively voted in during the 1990s. In other states, it varies. The street codes became a subject of the past. More up-and-coming gang affiliates had no street codes, so the older loyal gang members were the last of a dying breed. Even though they were involved in gang activity, it was more respect because of the disciplinary and attributes. Sad to say, murder rates set so high taught men to walk in their own lanes without worrying about the next man lane, respecting his circle. And usually, if a man got out of lane, stepping on someone's toes with bad intentions and an unruly unmanageable attitude, men of such valor became enshrined into the wall of statistics and casualties of a climbing but sad murder ratio. The 1980s preached respect. In the 1990s, respect was taught. In the year 2000, some states failed it, preaching and teaching those deadly attributes that determine the proof in the pudding of why some states are so far behind other cities who have suffered the travesty of murdering. And the results were so high and catastrophic that each generation can feel the effects of the many lost lives. I won't name any state, but you know who you are. If this is 2012 and you are competing against murder rates of the past, you have to be some of the dumbest born Negroes alive, repeating something that is almost depleted. The gang activities are nothing like back in the days, but fools are trying so hard while telling at the same time three-strike law changed the game. Even the older vets of 1990s have seen this coming because they were more political thinkers inclined to read the newspapers, intrigued to know what the law was plotting and what Civil Rights amendments were being stripped away. We were reading messages and books called *Behold the Pale White Horse, From Gods to Niggers, The King Alfred Plan*, quotes and prophecies from the Bible's book of Revelations. They reveal facts that we were taught during jail sentences. So many men knew what was coming. They informed those of us young and involved in gangs. The men were like us earlier in their lives, but they broke free of the mind shackles with life sentences they lived in prison, awaiting the arrival of some youth that was out of control in their own image before they had discovered the world dark hidden truths, with the purpose of being poor righteous teachers because of where they were. I call them what the world thinks of them, but the most sufficient teachings and information and thought come from the men anointed by God in prison to teach the mass of men because God needs teachers everywhere. And to reach the most wretched, the wretched must be converted. And living in the lion's den, you receive an up-close visual aspect of the educational perspective's view of so much more than the people in the outside free world of society, who live for the purpose of doing things, unseen or not, considered wrong because it's a job description. So they become an instrumental tool utilized in genocide, which they are too blinded with shackles of the mind to even notice how much they contributed to the cause with so much leverage hanging over their heads. They have become trapped in a one-track mind of thought, believing in if you wear a suit and tie, work with politics, talk, walk, nearly white, and live accordingly when you speak about lies and tell lies; then it is easier to believe it as a truth. Because the news say high-tech equipment we are programmed to conceive and believe it as a truth because the news broadcaster said it was high-tech equipment. That's actually what it was because they said so. I'm going along with it. A man sentenced to life with nothing but truth experienced, enduring and learning the ways of deception and teaching the incoming traffic of inmates. He has no creditability with anyone. Not even the black people who have achieved heights of notoriety in politics listen to his true

knowledge until they are sitting in a cell next to him after being caught for
overindulging in the money that they could've been investing back to help
decrease the crime rates. High-caliber words of confusion rambled together like
reading a phone bill with hidden fees. No average citizen understands them
because it's a design to make it too complicated to attempt until you get on board.
Simple is always easy, but complication keeps the confused outguessing, while
robbery is proceeding. Now you have it why so many politicians end up in prison
because the ones who get caught have to pay the cost. The politics, the gang, is all
in one with a license to kill. Quiet men attempt to change how they eat and feed
their families and expose their secrets. The gangs are just a product of our
environment, born and raised in America. There is not much to mention about
the decade or what identity 2000 had implicated, bringing a description of its own
identity to the table. Plenty of '80s and '90s are the generation of youth in the
streets, more lack luster in demeanor. They seem lazy, tired, senseless, lost,
dumbfounded, caught in the moment of now, not studying the decades before
them. They have no respect for the elders in the 1960s up until 1990s. More youth
in their ages knew how and had respect and were taught respect for the elders. If
you say anything about their disrespect, it can result in some sort of violence. They
seem to not be motivated, seeking knowledge at high rates. They don't seem to
notice the big changes coming, and they continue to have babies brought here
with what's going to occur, without evaluating the times. The year 2000 and beyond
is just simply the aftereffects and intertwined elements of each decade before it
sprinkled with the drive-bys of the 1920s. Many of the house Negroes of the 1960s,
the yes men who kept repeating, "yes you can beat me," saying yes to nearly
everything a white person requests, think about it. You know how you act when
white people are around. And black women, you know how your attitudes change
when you are helping white people, going all out; but when someone black pops
up, that nasty stinky fowl attitudes emerges, which sets us back further than any
senseless gang violence or black-on-black crime because you are detouring your
own people in the process. Some black dudes act like the black females with the
attitudes. And when you are not too busy trying to stick your chest out on the job
site and dealing with emotional issues like women, stop all the nail polishing, nail
biting, and gossiping. Leave it to the ladies. Unless you are discussing racism,
which is worldly advancement, stop worrying about how ugly the next man looks.
You have too many female tendencies and attributes. Elders stop the little boys'
game. My Tonka toy is faster because you have materialistic views, acting like a kid
on a big wheel on Christmas, riding around showcasing an ego as kids. The big
wheel doesn't sell itself. The kid does, and the men sell those broken dreams to
the boys whose agenda of life becomes distorted, without value of understanding
that man makes all things. The things don't make the men. Too many dudes ain't
teaching that so the boys are groomed and growing up, willing to sell out just
about for anything materialistic, even some grown men who are boys in mind.

1970s intertwined with black women who have stepped off the pedal of queens manship, as the black race pride the bearer of life, the lifeline, and life support of the race. Exposed, exploited with no respect at all, advertised as product or merchandise, the pimp has turned her into a two-dollar hoe without respect or pride. Look at a preschool and all the little girls. How many shall we allow to become whores and be pimped as prostitutes and be exploited as strippers, quick and ready to run to the clubs? Think of the places and industries clubs, stripper poles, the corners where whores stroll. The music videos of exploitation occur. Now put all the small little preschools girls in these spots. Now how explicit does it look to you to have the little black girls performing for you like a slave symbol? A little girl! Those are the elements we have intertwined in the year 2000, mixed like gumbo. 1920,1960, 1970, 1980, and 1990, each decade added to the compulsiveness of the year 2000 and beyond elements that make us as a race, figuring out what are we doing all so wrong that we can't get it together, adding more division. The street wars were reverting backward, and the gang affiliated is installed with so many different attributes of all the many elements of the many years that had passed him and came before him. Born in the '80s and '90s, they are clueless, who and what they are because of the way he represents himself, unaware that in reality, a buffoon in folly for foolishly going along with the way of the masses and not knowing the history behind the biggest design subplot, understanding every history event evolved because of some sort of action, having a reaction and tracing the years as far back as slavery, along with event, people, person, and thing the same way you were taught in third grade. Knowing about the gangs, you got to study all the events that occurred before it existence.

We didn't just all of a sudden become the worse race on the planet because of just pure coincidence. Something happened to modify and transformed our way of thought after slavery. Some people will begin to go back further than slavery because if you want to know, we were not always gangs of America. We were tribes, and before we were tribes, you must research and find out what you were. Black-skinned people, what importance does your people served the planet? As far as we can think, in history, we are taught that we were slaves from Africa, which developed an inferiority and slave mentality that makes you dependent on being ruled and controlled. Any man who discovers his true heritage and the profound facts of your being releases the shackles of the mind. You become free of the embodied prison, finding your family tree and the greatness in the color of your skin and the subplot of why you were so revered and rejected to know or read, finding out who you were and what great significance your people have contributed to the gift of this world, erasing the stereotyped inferiorities that were implanted mentally to create the man of year 2000 who is intertwined with all the other years combined to create what you have in existence as today's gang affiliate programmed machine that does exactly as the oppressors want.

"Red Rum, White Cops with Guns: The Boys in Blue Battle for Turf without the Slightest Clue"

The red represents the bloodshed, spilled all the innocents killed against their will, the lives lost in a brutal senseless war, mindless without a cost. Seek and destroy teams. Become void, a dream of a boy with everything to lose, uplifted in a world. Leaders are confused with misdirection. The boy loses direction, suffering wounds of war's infliction of contradictions. Which road is the correct road? He shall choose. For many victims have failed because of the simplicities of this corrupted world views and tainted atrocities. Daily he wakes, hoping there's a void in the place he lives, where the most catastrophic violence be. He talks, but he is urged to maintain silence. But he knows his goals to achieve peace don't produce or transpire if a man is quiet, disruptive in mind. Outburst a mind full with knowledge, like a fish out of water, craving and thirsty. What is worse? A man that finished last in a race, or a man determined to finish first? Red rum, Red rum! War intruding; bodies shot dead. Off with their heads, corpse bleeding. Bullets reach them like heat-seeking missiles. The bullets fly with ease through the skies, piercing the wind. How many innocents shall encounter Red rum imminently, face to face, encountering their end. Living life at fast forward, fast pace on the run, all life burden weighing a ton, then in reverse seems as if Red rum had won. Then I respected life more for Red rum nearly cost me dearly, noticing death would be a misery. Murder reversed is just Red rum, the illusion of confusion, deadly attributes of gang life. Alluring bullets fly by, blurring my visions, lost unable to make final vital decision until those missiles land with precision, inflicting contusions of an unruly lifestyle until I was reached and touched with retribution in my mind. Now I can conceive the thoughts of angels' intrusion, sending me the message, a well-taught lesson. When you're living life, don't cheat it twice. In the end, we all live and die, only to pay a price. Life at the end. How much good have you done when it began? Because we discovered all men cry. When at the end, all men die, unable to do it again. Some men reach high places in the sky; but the ones, the harder, they cry the more. They fry the worse of the earth, living a lie as if they didn't deserve to burn, taking lives without a concern or regret. They forgot to read or repent. Now they yearn, asking why absentminded as their souls fry time expired, condemned to that place everlasting, eternal fires. Get it right because in death, some of us don't get a chance twice. White cops driving inside police cars punched in on a clock, patrolling the ghettos as their shift starts with black Glocks. They aim shots at black dots: some good, some bad cops. Some have moral dispositions, and other have cruel and unusual intentions. In the '60s, their parents are involved in the Negro lynching. Like in school, they were taught to study and pay attention and bury the white sheets that created way too much heat. More improvised, discreet, and approachable, emphasize a difference in hate crime that is nonnegotiable. Throwing heat rocks, slaying two birds with one stone, hitting the block clearing the block, now its on take a choice get how you lived it, "black or chrome". Lullaby babies while tucking them in to a good-night bed song. Some thugs blast their heats back why other beat their feet. Crooks, Crips, thief, or criminals all get the message subliminal. A man is dead no matter what the color. When you're Bloods is red. All Criminals turn the concrete red, once a soul cant be save only one place which never grows satisfied with the taste for it is the loneliest place highly populated with many corpse erased off this earthly place deep deep in the ground is this where all the souls and bodies meet their demise of an unruly fate. The place that renders no births and no dates, just death and hate for mortals whom live so they can waist succumbed to an untimely place, in between never again to be seen. So life on the edge aint nothing but a thing!

Some crooks pop shots at cops' heads. Countless shot fired. Overkill feels the body cavity. Another suspect added to the senseless murder rate. A fallen expired casualty increased poverty zones, segregating living zones every day in the ghetto, a living war zone; while the white cops work eight hours and get to go home. Is it a crime to live in this jungle and remain humble without fumbling on a stumbling stone, because the lions fight turf wars for what block you live on? If you're white, you're right; but if you're black, your wrong, and the street hoodlums pointing a strap at your dome can't reach the phone in time to dial emergency. Dial tone is blank. In the spur of the moment, some minds go blank; while the crooks attempt to cash you out like an ATM in a bank. Some men won't wait for that dial tone. Prank instead of the bank, they shoot back until they clips are empty; and blank and the criminal elements can't think because hot hallows expressed a point which turned his criminal advancement, shimmering and shallow, because the bullet fragments were hollow tipped. Without thought, another mind was wasted. With disorderly conduct, he should have listen to his mother or got his ass whipped. Before he became a criminal and got his life took! Some say it's the white man I should fear, but it's the _____! That's doing all the killing here! Battered bruised, some turn blue because of a rough life they been through, alone and elusive, game conclusive lethal attributions, enemies reaping retributions. Evolving like spinning wheels of revolutions, havoc is what a man gets, who refuses to leave another in silence, in private. Rambo became violent when they refused to leave him in silence. They treated him like a migrant, for the sake to be alone on his island. Instead they should have chosen peace, over lead, with deep holes in the head. Blood is spilling, penetrating, soaking the bed like a sponge. Bullets enter your thoughts. Brain wave interruption makes niggas get dumb. In the city where I come from, they say you don't want none. When a man is alone, it's just that easier for Creeps to intrude his home, receiving scud missiles of projectiles, like erectile, dysfunction injunction, causing pain in the brain, entering the mind's conjuncture, like Chinese acupuncture. Rising to the occasion, amazing guns galore blazing, never phased, beating these rats in the race, at their own game and at a faster pace. When I'm done, their minds will never be the same, my mind tight like fresh braids, my words slice like a pair of new dope dealer blades. Cats take flight like bears in the night, lyrical words so far out of sight, like bright lights and raves, winter and caves, dirt and graves, souls that can't be saved, births without dates, milk without cake, a man without a face, feeling displaced; with no touch to feel, no look to see, that's when you realize you fools can't see me! Yet despite the truths, I ran with the teams of blue, realizing no matter how true the blue, the more fowler they become, until you revert back to picking up and living by the gun. If I'm wrong, then I'm right, with two swords by my side. If I tell, this be a lie. Nope! At their best, even Martin L. King had to die. To the world, Malcolm X was too complex. Why? Tell me why! A Negro emptied rounds into his chest. With Negroes in this world, like that, I'll rather sleep with a vest and walk around like Malcolm with a rifle and some Clips. Red, white, and blue equals the color of the flags. In these colors, they never retreat. Some rule and represents a cause without a beginning, without an end. Yet we all say one for all, all for one! We live by the gun. We stand tall because of the gun! We fall far because of the gun! Realizing it's not the gun at all. Because man made the gun. It didn't make the man. Probably stand confident without fear. It's the men behind the gun, the men behind the mask, behind the scenes with uncanny plans to cause havoc all across the land. Every place, every race, are all the same. If I was the creator from another planet, I think I would've left some of you Neanderthals trapped in a cave. No matter where you go, they all kill the same. Taking the gun away, they will use spoons to kill.

"ROLE CALL: CRIPS OF LOS ANGELES, CALIFORNIA"

Watts = CAC-95X7_WMC-99_HGWC-92_BTMC-97_BGMC-103_HTC-97_
WBLC—103_ TLGC-110_FTMC-105X7_PJWC-113_NHWC-109_FSWC-103_
BSWC-109_FCG-103 HSTWC._7STWC.

Compton = PVCC_MPCC_TPCC_KPCC_ADCC_SSCC_NBCC_FDCC_AGCC_
LBCC_NHCC_TZCC_OSCC_PBCC_STCC_ABCC_CPCC_SHCC_OPHCC_
OFHCC_CSCC_NACC_MACC_RSHCC_WLCC_DHCC_GTCC

South Central = HCG 52-59-74-83-92-94-107-112_ECG-1-59-62-66-
68-69-89-97—Q102—118-190_RSCNH_BGC-52-112_BCG113_
UGC_NHC111-46-48-55—112_RFC_H30C_MGC—65_ RAC-120_
MSMC-98-84_99MC_PBSC-95_PBHC_HTHC—104-78_BLGC
43GC_AGC40—53-88-116_KCG-87—116_83GC_42GC_87GC_97GC_
MAGC_HCC_ TGC_VPC_SVC_HTFC *DODGECC-HARVARDGC-MIDCC*
TZMC_MFGC_SYC_GGC_WBC_BSC_GTC_118GC_115GC_ESHC_
TFGC_PALMDALE-C SEASIDE-CRIPS_LANCASTER-CRIPS-_
SAC-TOWN-CRIPS-62DC_MODESTO-CRIPS_ SANDIEGO-CRIPS_
FRESNO-CRIPS-PJC_SAN-BERDINO-CRIPS_CGC_44GBC_GYC
SANJOSE-CRIPS_SANFRANCISCO-BANNING_RIVERSIDE-CRIPS_
BAKERSFIELD—ONTARIO-CRIPS_ ORIGINAL-VALLEY-GANGSTER-
CRIPS_FONTANA-VALLEY-CRIPS PACIOMA-CRIPS_ALTADENA-CRIPS_
DUERTE-CRIPS_PASADENA-CRIPS WEST-COVINA 90-CRIPS

Gardena = SGC_PBC_ LYNWOOD= NHC_PSC_CAC_POGC_WBC_
INGLEWOOD= RAC-102_IVC-119_LCG_TCG_WGC

Long Beach = RTC_ICG_BBC_FCHC_MMC_BMC_ABC_LNHC_OHC_R80C_SOS

Pomana = 357C_AMC_GTC_WSMC_SSVC_STC_ECC200_PASADENA=RCG_
ABC_DRC

"DIFFERENT STATES IN AMERICA: CRIPS AND BLOODS CAN BE LOCATED, INCLUDING OTHER CONTINENTS"

New Jersey—Texas—Las Vegas, Nevada—Denver, Colorado—Portland, Oregon—New York—Philadelphia—Phoenix, *Arizona—Seattle, Washington—Kansas City, Kansas; Little Rock, Arkansas; St. Louis, Missouri-Memphis; Tennessee—Cleveland, Ohio—Oklahoma—Birmingham, Alabama—Mississippi—New-Orleans—Louisiana— Atlanta—Georgia—North Carolina—South Carolina—Los Angeles, California—Florida— Detroit—Michigan—Minnesota—West, Virginia—Pittsburgh, Pennsylvania—Virginia— Nebraska—Wisconsin—Iowa-Kentucky. CONTINENTS = LONDON, JAMAICA, ALASKA, SOMOAN ISLANDS, HAWAII, PHILIPEANS, BELIZE, BRAZIL, HATIA*

"Role Call: Bloods Gangs of Los Angeles, California"

(Compton, Watts, South Central, Inglewood, Lynwood, Pasadena, Pacioma, Palm Dale = CPT-135-PIRU_CPT-FRUIT-TOWN-PIRU_CPT-TREE-TOP-PIRU_ HOLLY-HOOD-PIRU_LWD-LIME-HOOD-PIRU_LWD-MOB-PIRU_ CPT-WEST-SIDE-PIRU_CPT-LUEDES-PARK-PIRU_CPT-EAST-SIDE-PAIN_ CPT-ELM-ST-PIRU_CPT-WATER-FRONT-PIRU_CPT-CEDAR-BLOCK-PIRU_ NEIGHBORHOOD-PIRU_CAMPANELLA-PARK-PIRU_ LWD-CROSS-ATLANTIC-PIRU_CENTER-VIEW-PIRU_WATTS-CIRCLE-CITY- PIRU_30-PIRU_40-PIRU_SCOTT-DALE-PIRU_92-WATTS-EAST-SIDE-BISHOP_92- BEE-BOP-WATTS-BLOODS_WATTS-HACIENDA-VILLAGE-BLOODS_POMANA- 456-PIRU_52-PUEBO-BISHOP-BLOODS_VAN-NESS-GANGSTER-BLOOD_ ATHENS-PARK-BLOODS_FRUIT-TOWN-BRIMS_NEIGHBORHOOD-20'S- BLOOD-OUTLAW-20'S_62-HARVARD-PARK-BRIMS_MAD-SWANN-BLOODS- 84-79-77_BLACK-P-STONE-BLOODS_30-BLACK-STONE-PIRU_56-BLOOD- STONE-VILLAIN_MILLER-GANGSTER-BLOOD_PACIOMA-PIRUS-BLOOD_ ING-QUEEN-ST-BLOODS_WATTS-BOUNTY-HUNTER-BLOODS-CARSON- SOMOAN-WARRIOS_89-FAMILY-SWAN-BLOODS_ING-CRENSHAW-MAFIA- GANGSTER_INGLEWOOD-FAMILY-BLOODS_DENVER-LANE-BLOODS_ ING-AVENUE-PIRU-GANG_PASADENA-DENVER-LANE-BLOODS_ PASEDENA-SUIGLEY-LANE-BLOODS_CENTANELLA-PARK-FAMILY_ WEST-COVINA-MOB-PIRU_CPT-151-PIRU_SD-SKY-LINE-PIRU.

Most Bloods and Pirus gangs occupy the same areas where Crips gangs are found, from every city to states, even in other continents, one doesn't exist without the other, the role of evil twin brothers.

"Year 2000: Change of Tides"
The New Millennium of Bloods and Crips
"No Holds Barred," "No Rules," "No Street Codes," "No Exceptions"!

Decades after the peace treaty of 1992 between the two warring rival and bitter enemies, Crips and Bloods, kids were able to walk outside and play in the playgrounds. They were held hostage, becoming the headquarters and launching zones of attacks for most Crips and Bloods, also utilized as the places where the two groups would meet separately to discuss political gang views and initiate disciplinary action toward supposedly violators or just simply for amusement and sharpening ones defensive skills. The children who played in the playground before the treaty risked being struck by stray bullets in retaliations or results of gang warfare; therefore, the playgrounds were void of children and were replaced by gang affiliates. Unlike the unstructured, rebellions, renegade Crips who normally dived in headfirst, in an all-out, all-in crash course collision derby between other Crips factions. Shoot first; ask questions later. The Crips throughout the years became their own worst enemies. With many Blood gangs far and distant, the only way other Crips gangs were able to gain stripes, or street creditability was for them to engage in all-out wars with other Crips sets that were closer to them. Even if they had attempted to avoid local feuds, it was just a matter of time before the two factions would engage in all-out wars. When two groups with similar views occupy the same terrain, disputes are common, with collisions becoming regular with no space or elbow room, disorderly, obnoxious youth cause, conflicting egotistical behavior and the demand of notoriety becoming more like a pissing contest. Escalating over mostly women, pride, money, and the mechanism of who can annihilate who the fastest becomes the initiative. This is the result of so many Crips feuding because of simple-minded childish acts of proving something non important but feeding one's ego. The Bloods, though they were outnumbered at times because of the feuding Crips wars against each other, utilized the feuds, wearing blue and going out on missions and inadvertently causing various numerous Crips factions to engage in war while they were in covert mode, waiting to receive the damage report. Sometimes this plan backfired because if that Bloods sets that had caused the two Crips sets to collide resided anywhere near those two Crips sets, infused in a sabotage-type war, without any suspicion. Because of how LA gang wars are fought, all surrounding gangs are normally attacked; engaged in all-out war, and every rival enemy turf within a fifty-mile radius, they become suspect targets! Despite the accusations and the whispers circulating throughout the streets, further fueling the battles in the same way a spectator sits at the front row during a prize fight, waiting to see the end results of who gets knocked out! Both gangs were familiar with trick used to gain advantages in casualties, many methods, and tactics applied, refusing to become buffoons or laughingstocks or clowns for not knowing who the true instigator behind the ploy actually turned out to be. Terms being drastic! Revenge, lethal, and casualties—a must. All enemy hoods are targeted with precision.

How ironic it is when a group celebrates after instigating a bout between two rival gangs who happen to be opposing enemies, clash because of calculated sabotage, putting two arch foes against one another. Then out the thin blue sky, they become victims of gang-related shootings, the result of an action playing out the California way, the rule of thumb when a shooting occurs. The true questions remain unknown. How many people had been shot beforehand? Why and what was the actual motive? Every shooting has a point of origin and a boiling point! Which caused un-relentless retaliations shootings, with a chain reaction effect. Like dominoes, each one has to touch the next in order for the next domino to fall flat because of the force of the first domino affecting all the other; and that's how California gang wars are initiated along with many gangs world wide. Throughout the entire state, this effect has become a plague! One turf war creates a domino effect of many engaged hood conflicts throughout the entire City of Angels! The Bloods throughout the late 1960s up until the millennium change of the year 2000 were one in all, all in one! The Bloods were united, so many years on hand. They had always solved minor conflicts. They had squashed many beefs. Prior to this upscale change that were results of two affiliated Bloods boxing or having a verbal disputes over a common female companion that two allies were involved in some sort of love triangle affair, unlike the Crips who would jump in headfirst, thirsting for bloodshed, eager to shoot it out, with a Viking or pirate like attitude. It was rare and seldom that a Crips set would squash minor beefs with any other hood. The Bloods on the other hand were more organized and mature; they never had such catastrophic issues that resulted in all-out wars with other Bloods gangs. Somehow they settled their indifferences before things got totally out of control. Bloods could have numerous house parties without one single incident. The Crips are known more for being party poopers, crashing parties! Almost every group gathering, they attempt to mingle and relax, networking, meeting other members of Crips from different sectors; but of course, as usual, it ended with some unknown male or female suffering from some sort of fatal gunshot wound, because of some jealous and envious individuals seeking to simply gain street recognition. The consolidation of unity, which bound the Bloods' structure, would weaken. An infusing change developed between the Bloods during the mid-1990s. The Bloods of Denver Lane had an all-out feud with the Pirus of Compton. This conflict would initiate a domino effect of wars between the two Damu sets, destroying their unity, which held them strong and cohesively. Prepared to combat the Crips, the Pirus took a page from the notorious Hoover Crips book, who had disassociated themselves from the letter C and called themselves Hoover Criminals. All the while, some Hoovers continued to wear blue and use terms such as cuzz. They had become known as the first Crips to change its colors to orange, red bandannas, signifying their sincerity of being Crips and Bloods killers. In similarities, the Pirus began to write on the walls in gang-related terms, called "wall banging," a simple sign of "warning before destruction"! The walls usually tell all. Police use them for Intel, and gangs use them to excite wars, also to determine whether or not it is safe to travel in certain areas. That might be heading into crash course collisions!

"Clash of the Titans." The terms Bloods (BK), Crips (CK) killer. Pirus began slurring, defaming former Bloods gang allies, with insults, identifying them as slobs, to deprive them, and disassociating themselves with the letter B or Bloods. The Pirus preferred the reference of being identified as only Pirus, replacing the color red with burgundy, which had always been their primary bandanna color, worn by all Pirus, used to give them street verification. Many other gangs on both sides of the fence—Crips, Bloods—choose very peculiar bandannas colors. Hustler Crips utilized "green bandannas." Santana Block and Hat Gang Watts Crips shared in common "black bandannas." Compton Ave, Beach Town, Acacia Block Compton Crips choose "sky blue bandannas." Fudge Town and Nut Hood Watts Crips choose "brown bandannas." Lime Hood Piru choose "lime green bandannas." Front Street Watts Crips choose "royal blue." Watts Baby Loc's Grape St Crips choose the purple flag monicar as a perfect fit. Over all, the original colors remained: "navy blue" and "red" as a primarily universal color for both gangs. In retaliations of the slurred statements written on walls in gang code, our form of Morse code, communication without using the phone lines. The Bloods responded to the insults, returning fire, referring to the Pirus as Dirus, a derogatory term used as disrespect by both gangs who were former allies. In the mind of the immature gang, affiliated words spoken or wall-banged can result in fatal repercussions. Every method applied, every antic involves calculated thoughts of sabotage. Verbal insults are threats that become promises, replying to incidents of casualties, increasing the valor of indirect shootings during war. Becoming magnified (3X), multiplied, more exclusively intense, dramatized because of street publicity and notoriety, word of mouth spreads along with false rumors; and small minor disagreements evolve into all-out, full-throttled friction between two indifferent groups with one common motive. Other Bloods and Pirus gangs tried to become mediators in this soon-to-be war. After occurring, deaths and multiple retaliated shootings had pursued the first casualty of war that initiated the Denver Lane versus Pirus Beef. Soon after, the many efforts to disengage this beef caused more conflicts between the mediators, which resulted in all Bloods gangs to take the sideline. Crips got word of the beef, finding it amazing that the unified, more calculated Bloods were feuding with the Pirus; and it was hilarious for Crips to view Bloods wall-banging Pirus killer (PK). And the Pirus in return would write Bloods killer (BK) or simply 187, a police terminology for murder. This was unordinary, after all the years of annihilating Crips together. The Bloods and Pirus turned on each other, the same way Crips had been doing for nearly twenty plus years. The change of the millennium looming, with the three-strike law in effect, twent-five years to life for any third offensive crime, murder off top, any criminal received a quarter of a century off top. The game was changed, and the contagious snitching that had plagued all neighborhoods was in motion. This would separate the boys from the men, also allowing most cowardly lions to come to the forefronts with the threat of dialing 911. In similarities to hitting your baby brother, he threatens you that if you hit him again, he is going to run and tell Mother. You become less reluctant to punch your baby brother. Most gang-affiliated next generation, new-millennium thugs, excited events, going out doing dirt, committing crimes, then hiding so that the retribution could not be inflicted, causing more beefs on the inside of interior groups, creating division within gangs who were groomed and grew up as family. As soon as things became too intense and overly heated, these guys knew that the guys they had been dealing with were too much for them to handle, instead of colliding and reap becoming a statistic of war. After instigating, provoking, and ruffling some feathers of the older school last of the dying breed more loyal street persona, Thanks to the new innovative three-strike law. Individuals in gangs used the laws to their advantage. If they couldn't beat you, someone would drop a dime and had you arrested and facing the three strikes to life. With the rise of new warfare, fought by cowards upon retaliation, these guys would threaten other guys who they were very afraid to face or confront that if they had done anything wrong to them, the police would subsequently receive information related to past crimes committed. Home boys that grew up best friends and went to school together, smashing on rival enemies who attempt to invade the turf's boundaries, sharing women and clothes, while uplifting each other out of poverty. Times changed, and friends begin killing each other. It became the era of the new increased "No motto," "No honor among thieves," "No rules," "No exceptions"! The street code of the old had died out with the last of the dying breed, the truest soldiers of Los Angeles had produced. Not taking nothing away from the loyal realist of the newer generation, but nowadays, this breed is very much a lot more different than before. Even though we paved the way, the respect factor was highly enforced, because the lifestyle was much more serious. Life wasn't a joke. There was nothing to play around with when the streets conducted the no-man, no-mercy rule with the iron fist. Men lived inside their lanes and respected people they didn't know because any insult or slur could cause you your life Respect was far most demanded by everyone and given without a doubt. We also became more politically inclined during our era because of racial profiling and police harassment. We achieved negotiating a peace treaty and an uprising to combat the racism, taking a stand for a common important liberal goal to seek justice for the people. We were attempting to breach the wars with applying unity inside the urban communities. Now in today's era, 2012, with the incline of race wars, I can't believe how foolish individuals are pursuing and continuing to apply bullets rather than unity. The Bloods have been engaged in street wars with so many Crips for so long. They have begun to emulate the characteristics and traits of "me-against-the-world view," mimicking how the Crips shoot and kill each other! Bloods are beefing with Bloods and so forth. Killing wars between the factions have become the new millennium norm. The day the Bloods kill each other, the signs are pivotal proof of revelation. We look for world wars in other continents, waiting for the clues to find proof of revelations prophecies. The proof is in your face every day in this "United States of

America World War 3." It has been active for nearly twenty plus years in the forms of gangs. The wars are directly under our noses, revealed and concealed. The rumors of wars and the death tolls climb year to year and accumulate, while at the same time, newer type crimes are turning into full all-out race wars in urban minority communities involving blacks and Latinos. Believe it or not, the Bible speaks of these things! Race has always been the unspoken. Let's not discuss its topic. Yet every day it is a vital part of our lives. Because of living conditions, hidden agendas of segregation, discrimination factors, poverty lines with intentional moral displacement served on a higher platform but perceived much lower below the pitcher's mound, questions of racial ethnicity navigated and were used like a compass to stereotype, and discrimination was utilized as prevention of intellectual gain and stability of liberty and profound accomplished achievements of the culture. Apex contributions are deceptively overlooked as underachievers, inferior, nonexistent, not equal, or considered in the ranks of high-profiled forefathers of attribution. Reckoning because of the rise and achievements, accomplishment of invention, innovativeness of the Afro American in America somehow becomes less mentioned or highlighted as a great task related to the Africans, much more known throughout history, labeled as slaves with an atrophy to depict inferiorities indirectly, insinuation of deceptiveness, of demoralizing genocide, without taking full direct blame, while taking full direct creditability for the achievements. In Egypt and discovery of America and all events of importance that have shaped the world as it is today, proclaiming full accountability for all that is good and that which is not lies solely on the minorities, developing inferior personalities as regards not feeling appreciated, belonging to a race with such great importance, with the teachings surrounded, highlighted only around one group of people solely claiming to have been the first and innovators and everyone else, lesser or unequal, last to none, which proves since the beginning of civilization's existence. Race wars have always been a part of mankind's dark past. Some race group or individuals have always played the role of teacher's pet (a slave), while even in the Bible, rather it be the truth, these are distorted facts. Masters and slaves are mentioned and documented! Segregated areas in the olden world where some races had never seen a black man or woman before, which is total proof of how segregated times were. The fight for land and the simplicities of ignorance to dominate and control others. War has always succeeded humankind's greed and thirst to rule as all high and mighty and conquering this marathon's urination contest, of who can water hose the land the furthest, while urinating on ourselves and everyone else in the process to be number 1. Thousands of years later, those same traits have been passed down and taught on great scales and smaller scales, which defines the demeanor and attributes of the persona and mentality adopted by some affiliated Bloods and Crips, too young to remember history or too dumbfounded by inferiorities, of other proclaimed superior races because of the highlighted motive teachings. They have not studied about the true realities of self-worth and the hidden contributions that liberate the shackles of the slave-depicted stereotype mind of the Negroes. How it was thousands of years before the 1900, the twenty-first century. And how the 1980s could compare with the years dating back when Egypt ruled! Some young Afro-Americans were not born yet. If you have been too damn committed in the hoods, unable to travel, try it. Then you will realize how populated blacks were in California, because of the southern migration in the early twenty-first Century (1900s). On every block, there approximately exist entire families of black ethnicities. We are highly populating these zones. My true intentions are not meant to appear racist. I'm simply trying to paint a visual picture of perception, allowing the mind to travel into the past and back into the future, comparing the facts of history's past events of all races who some were inadvertently misidentified as innovators and all subplots, transpiring without full definition of reason, events that have depicted and affected stereotyping the people of this era, complying to inferiority. Why race has always been at the forefronts. I can remember while growing up as a Child in Watts on the streets where I lived, maybe two families were Hispanic. We accepted them with open arms and got along fairly well. Now thirty years later, we have nearly annihilated ourselves to almost extinction with other additional factors that you must place the pieces together as a gang affiliate, seeking redemption, finding solution in the quest of enlightenment, researching and opening the past of what happened to the Africans. You will have to go back, starting with the Bible. The most detrimental, defined facts are in the book of knowledge. And you will be able to understand so many answers to your questions and compare other facts that exist in other books along with knowing the things that occur today. You will find so much truth on how important blacks are! Without searching, reading, and studying history, we remain the sole purpose of our own demise. When a man does not know true world history, he is bound to repeat it. Stop sitting in the city in your state, afraid to leave. If you can't afford to travel, use your mind to read and travel out of the state of California, or whatever state or city you may be confined to. Stop babysitting the hood, observe how in Atlanta all the beautiful black sisters in Chicago beautiful black women in Alabama, New Orleans, Texas, Detroit, and Baltimore. These states all have crime rates, but if you go there, man, it's so much different than California. It's a more higher percentage and ratio of blacks that populated and occupy many states in America, even in different continents such as Brazil, Columbia, Belize, and Africa. Languages are different, but the black race is diverse and in almost every place where snow falls and the grass grows green, even in Great Britain. The truest fact is that even in London, all around the earth, race riots have brewed and have been stimulated through bigotry and racial brutality! We must master and figure out why have we been the primary target depicted for thousands of years across the globe and why? In the early 1950s up until 1980s, blacks were everywhere. Every block was predominantly black in the state of California. Because of the highest murder rates seen in one state, I define a term associated with the blacks that pick up, pack up, and move out. Black flight! With force, many blacks have relocated in the grave, prison, and other states: the renovated new black flight, escape from Los Angeles initiated in the early 1990s effectively orchestrated in 2012, the result of population depletion. If you were born in the 1990s or mid-(1980s, most likely you think it was always predominantly Hispanic in California. If you haven't been informed or took time to study the facts of history, you and your peers or the last line of survival of a nearly depletion ongoing in the state of California, statistics indicate every decades, times change. And if your generation doesn't unite, give or take, 2022 will not be so pleasant for the Afro-American in the state of California. Don't let your egos defeat you. Know your history. Egypt fell populations million. Rome fell population millions. Human history is world history. Knowing any man's mistakes, you can avoid repeating it! I was born in 1975, and things had changed from being all populated white areas to almost highly populated black ghettos overnight. One state example is that California went from being all white populated with zero blacks nearly and with white flight. The black population increased. Now in California, the population is decreasing, reversing; and the black population is at the very bottom of the totem pole, next to white Caucasians, in the state of California. Hispanics are outnumbering blacks and whites combined! The black need to just go outside and look around and compare the stats of populations of the 1980s to 2012 and determine how long it will take for the depletion to become complete myself I determined every decade's big changes occur, so I approximate ten years, give or take, it will be difficult to locate blacks in California. Some most likely will migrate to other parts of California, where less racial crimes are prohibited, and more blacks reside or some blacks will completely move to other states that are mostly populated with blacks. The black Californians must put aside the big egos and stop thinking it can't happen to us because it's already in the mix and the gangs with huge numbers the big gangs that are Crips and Bloods who are not worried because they think they too deeply so they are careless about unity. They are more concerned about "me against the world." When the population is wiped nearly out, you will become like the First Street East Coast, surrounded! Ask them how they continue to exist. Just adding a little gang history in the mix to paint a perfect picture of an example, facts of not repeating history. With population nearly depleted, how will you recruit? You will go from having ten thousand members to only five thousand, from five thousand to only two thousand. If you don't believe, study race riot facts of the early 1900s. How some races increased from 73,000 to 743,000 in just a decade and some races southern States where lynching occurred regularly along with hate crimes and race riots, resulting of black families being burned out, with no place to live, nowhere to go, forced to migrate to places where the blacks were highly populated. Race populations decreased from five hundred thousand to nearly ten thousand almost overnight, a percentage ratio of 490,000 people that vanished from one place. For example, out of five hundred people, only one hundred were left standing at an 10 percent extinction, migration ratio. That tough guy act is irrelevant without brains over steel. As a teenager, I was informed long ago that times will get so hard that only a thinking man shall survive. We always as youth think we are smarter than the average bear, thinking we would use tactics and outmaneuver our predecessors, such as the street legends Nicky Barnes, Freeway Rick, Big Meechy, Frank Lucas, and the list goes on and continue adding a long list of names of all the black men of the ghettos with ten- and twenty-year runs. All succumbed with the same result. With time change, the sophistication of technology advanced becoming so complex, you can't even have a private conversation without spilling some sort of vital information that will add you to that famous list of the Incredible of the ghettos. In 1995, Goodie Mobb said, "Who's that peeping through my window?" What reverse technology gangs have to combat their freedom? Brains and unity and the reluctance to kill each other! Anything else you will simply be playing Russian roulette with your life! So the big egotistical mind-set that during your generation you can't be touched or depleted as a race as long as you fight inwardly with a population of five hundred thousand depleted, yet you continue the Crips versus Bloods wars, thinking that it's not impossible to vanish with race wars going on, and you're outnumbered 1,500,000 to only 500,000. For example, while your numbers decline, their numbers incline. Many factors are involved. Your race is migrating outward, and your foes are migrating inward, advancing every day. How can you overcome such odds without becoming allies such as the 1992 peace treaty and a race unified as one division destroys and unity wins. Ask the Indians what does "divide and conquer mean"? Strength is in numbers! A monkey said it in the movie *The Planet of the Apes*: "One Monkey alone weak, but all Monkeys together strong" My point is are we not smarter than a fifth grader? Are we not smarter than a primitive primal ape? When we stand erect as Afro-Americans. Being young, we are blessed with natural abilities, so I know for a fact that a young man will fail at leading the masses because of his immaturity and logical thought process, but their minds are not fully developed. So they think day to day, prematurely playing chest with fatal life moves that affect the game, causing the queen to be captured, abducted because they think ill rational and sentimental. Good in the battlefield, but his mental advancement is affected with personal complex issues that will affect the pawns around him. One bad apple spoils the bunch. Proof, for example, study the Panther and the U.S. organization allowing themselves to be pit against each other, disputes over who achieved and received notoriety resulting in "divide and conquer." Resulting in the demise of both groups, what remains today is a vacuum of buffoons, some not, but the majority transformed into the gangs of today; and all they have left behind is their story for us not to repeat! Example in kingdoms. When a kingdom had fallen, the queen was captured, and all the women alike were raped and became slaves. Does that sound familiar? Think back to Africa's history and the 400 plus years of slavery in America. Go back further than that to nearly

1300 BC. How many times has that same result repeated itself? A known fact is that history revolves and continues to repeat past events. Just when we think we have become civilized, all it takes is the rise and fall of an empire, reaching a peak point that which rises must fall! The law of gravity always pulls down. When you can't evolve, achieving all accomplishments, one can only fall after rising! The Afro-American race can be considered as an empire without unity. Gravity is the outcome result! What upsets me is that I have family affiliated with the Park Village Compton Crips and associates of many Crips and Bloods gangs. Whenever I hear them speak about newly enticed neighborhood conflicts with local Crips or Bloods factions at war, I compare it with a nation falling like a monumental empire such as Rome or Egypt! Not only does this happen in one state. Some states have endured many decades before. For example, such as Chicago, with high gratitude, being the city with the highest murder rate for bragging rights, foolishly repeating history, annihilating itself and succumbing to the same interior motives of depletion that have occurred in California, give or take in two decades maybe less, if the murder rates soars and migration occurs, and the migration of foreigners begin to flood the state of Illinois as it did during the 1919 Chicago Red Summer Race Riots. It could happen! The same effect occurs with almost the same calculated results of depletion! I find it despicable how many blacks feud and war with senseless, immoral direction, decreasing their own numbers without thought with past events, not familiarizing themselves how the past became detrimental to all great empire's demise, sentimental attributes of inflicting casualties upon the short-handed black race that are unraveled in an ongoing demographic conflict of racially motivated intentions that pits civilians against civilians, where the normal targets becomes ethnic groups, people who have the slightest clue about gang warfare. The streets become unsafe for any and every one walking when these type of events occur. No one wins after both sides lose lives. The saying you kill one, I'll kill two will go on, just the same as all the wars beforehand. Who can shoot children, grandmothers, and grandfathers because of race with pure all-out intentions to demise a race? When we all have family, if you can, then believe it. If you can be heartless! Without remorse, it can also happen to you! When you have no more enemies, then you yourself become your own worst enemy. And the people who look like you shall engage in conflict because of that sentimental envy and hate that devours all competitors. I have written gang views not to encourage you to indulge in all-out wars. To know the beast, you must have lived inside the belly of the beast. These facts are simply to educate the sleep walkers who jump into beefs. Because of my ethnicity, my soul targets are to reach my people. Even though some men are older, their views are tainted, not all but most. And with my gift, I write to those who read to highlight all faults involved in this ongoing war with poor unrighteous teachers. Some of us sit high in position, lacking to provide support, but pushing more for a vote; while the people of renown say we have no-more leaders when we were all leaders. We become too settled with everything we have gained individually. Our unity is shattered because we have become hungry for the almighty dollars, materials of this world, selfish-hearted with a gang banger mentality or a street thug's atrocities. Some politicians are more criminal than an actual criminal, as long as we see our self well off. All we ever do is talk cheap with fancy words with no quality or efforts, marching in nonviolent peace struggles for a week and back off to their safe haven in the peaceful suburbs, while the less fortunate are left behind to endure the wars in this menacing ghetto until there is no one else left in modest society for the land will become lawless. We only focus on successful ventures of me. In the process, we are the biggest consumers, buying everyone's product or merchandise. How can we help black owned while black owned sticks it to you, overcharging the black number 1 consumer in the world? No one buys black product at a high inconsiderate rate. That defines why most black people shop outside the black lines of distributions. More blacks go into business and out of business before the business is launched off the ground. Check the stats. Do your research, and you will agree that we as black people, we buy everything everyone else promotes, and if we do achieve getting some sort of business launched, we overcharge black customers, which in return makes you lose profit, customers, and business, not thinking long-term cost for you. When you have the mind-set that one customer, money isn't important and continue to overcharge the most important, all-reliable black consumer. You lose. We all lose, because we just are not simply understanding how we have become our own worse problem, segregated in our efforts, selfish in our hearts, doomed by ourselves because we are to comfortable with all we are allowed to accomplish in America. If our rights are becoming nonexistent, then we are nothing but just simple slaves again do to our own demise. We are innovative people, but sometimes greed is an interior motive, with the thought of creations! Of gangs manifested and the mere effort put forward to build and put the bricks, together laying the foundation of America. We are here to stay. We are the black-tainted secret that have done so much for this country. Without us, some things wouldn't be. Just think of all the things we have taught the world, adding some soul and humor sprinkled with pizazz. It's time for us to get back up to where we were heading during all that marching in the 1960s. "United we stand, divided we fall"! If we were slaves almost 175 years ago, how great were we? What caused us to become slaves as a punishment from God? Being of mankind and the Negroid race, are we just repeating history with our inward fighting just as our African Ancestors had done before us in tribal African Warfare? Thus, we sold out our entire country because of ignorance and lack of coming together as one combined. Only Chaka Zulu achieved this great accomplishment. Have our larger-than-life boisterous egos always been our Achilles' heel? Not to exclude our pleasure before business attitudes, or did we adopt that trait after becoming Americanized? Because some of our attributes are simply because of slave displacement and genetic breeding of an order executed by the slave master.

A PRODUCT BRANDED FROM THE GHETTO

Growing up in the ghettos, I was transformed from an innocent church boy in choirs, beating drums, to hanging on drug-infested street corners, transporting and slanging drugs. I have big dreams of becoming a street legend on the run, elevating, climbing up the charts as public enemy number 1. I am the next American nightmare, the local street thug, evading police sirens, toting and shooting guns, without a license to kill or be killed. I witnessed this ghetto violence, little kids dying. My heartbeat has become silent. In my eyes, there were no more tears, just an empty space. Where tears once formed, it has now become a dormant place, with no more feelings of emotional disposition. My dysfunctional demeanor transitioned into a mentally disturbed menace. I became heartless and vicious, a young boy considered a young misfit with no direction, but somehow always on a criminal path, awaiting my next victim. My rage and passion is in heat when guns blaze and blast. It is my mission as the local street thug (a.k.a. "the Silent Assassin"). Smoking and drinking were an everyday solution, allowing us an escape route to avoid the daily violence of this ghetto chemical warfare pollution. The American nightmare, homicidal, gang-affiliated serial killers, the menace of society, misled without sanity or sobriety, the black men in America, a product of a dying breed. Like a slave, emancipated and freed; like a seed, planted and uprooted, indeed. The last man standing is just simply the last black man standing of the almost depleted species, fallen from black-on-black infliction, hung juries of contradiction, almost like a slave hunt and another Negro lynching, falsified pretense of law and order corrupted jurisdiction. A hang man hung from a tree, put through the loop of no rules of engagement. My life was judged by those lighter than me, those racists who were whiter than me, leading this immoral marathon that was demographically designed, a ghetto trap, a ghetto snare for the black-eyed coons, on the run from a society that consumes, like the tale of a black man and a black lagoon, who they say with his life of procreation evolved from a measly baboon. Does this seem taboo? Is it true that some blacks emulate whites and everything they do? So is that why they say monkey see monkey do? When blacks have oppressed more blacks than white people do, when a Negro calls you an Uncle Tom, is that directed toward you? If you are black and from the ghetto or the distant suburbs, does this identify you? Targeting your own people and acting as if you had the slightest clue? Dissatisfaction increases crimes committed because of lack of development. Infractions create confrontations, leading to demoralizing displacement. Negative actions beget positive results of resolution without revolutions! The tribal instinct that is not extinction, freedom and liberation of a black man's mind expanded. Enslavement creates the barriers of mental shackles. Breaking free like a dynamite or grenade that goes boom! Top of the peak like an avalanche that consumes, swept up like a broom that cleans a room. The effects of a strong black man more catastrophic than a typhoon, neutrons, and protons and nukes that go boom, creating the spark in the mind that becomes bright and loud, this systematic mushroom, a misty dark cloud. The brain is the knowledge, which is knowing what you can perceive. It is that which must be achieved! Keep your starlight bright for that dark matter, and your matter is the facts. You are king, so be proud to be black. "They say the blacker the berry, the sweeter the juice!"

Discussing the facts of gang wars, ancient African tribal war, slavery, and the design of most criteria that is orchestrated to cause prevention of advancement throughout certain specific political, public areas in America, specifically for the reason of hindering racial barriers because of the covert and secretively bias agendas that has become high tech and modernized, which racism has changed with the newer times. As long as a few blacks are allowed to advance, then the Illusion beforehand prevents the argument that racism is alive, along with discrimination. And with those few blacks selected and allowed power position, they become dumbfounded and agreeable, accustomed in their new position as an employee, so these blacks are actually being secretly and deceitfully coerced to permit black-on-black crimes behind the desk. They are in some sort of office or field of employment despite the fact you are promoted branch manager, CEO, supervisor, or even president. Truth is you are just the poster child, puppet on a string, being strung along by someone behind the scene. Behind the mask exists a true puppet master who have conquered a most advanced way of inflicting his/her hatred toward Jews, blacks, and other ethnicity backgrounds. As long as you are employed, you continue to be a slave in his eyes, carrying out his/her obscene agendas of deception using you in a ploy to deny the existence of racism while putting one against the other, adopting to the modern times. During slavery, they were called house Negros; field Negros; and the infamous, most hated black slave catchers, who blacks hated more than their master, because these black men enjoyed oppressing and whipping other blacks. So comprehend and visualize that during today's time, the hate is alive and strong but just modernized, discreetly and secretly. Thus, the bigots have realized that with deception and allowing certain Negro power positions, they can sit back collectively and observe from afar as black-on-black crime is initiated on two different scales: the streets have gangs, and everywhere else has the modest so-called black civilians that are in a sense worst then any affiliated gangs because they are highly educated with master's and bachelor's degrees. There is the commitment to oppression while denying or in denial that certain agendas exist, directed and targeting minority groups of color. These people make gangs look like choir boys because behind the scenes, their judgment and actions have destroyed lives of many blacks. They have enforced rules or regulations that could have been avoided. The only purpose meant is to hinder or cause infliction. The African American has no country nor do the original descendants of Africa have continents! Japanese rule and control Japan; China, Russia, Europe, North Korea rule their own countries, Africa is ruled and controlled by "Great Britain." We don't even own our own place of creation because of our big, egotistical, boisterous ways and pleasure placed before business, inward fighting and will to sell each other out. We are at the very bottom of the totem pole. Those races seek to help each other despite the rules and regulations. They are the rulers of their own countries, and they are considered mega powers of the world. Despite how dirty their hands would get with blood, only the victors get the spoils! Joined as one, "the United States" became united and fought for the liberation of declaration to become a free country, breaking free of the tyranny, liberating themselves from being ruled by "the French and Great Britain." The solution they discovered is "united you stand, divided you fall!" The Civil War was fought for currency. The slaves were like kilos of narcotics an high commodity, on demand, and a very exclusive profitable market. Some say the fight was for the liberation of the Negro man. Truth is, other objectives stood first and foremost, such as buying up land or simply taking the land in order to build railroads and also to conquer the south as one country united with just one ruler. Thus, the men of the south were disagreeable, ruthless, and renegades who wanted nothing to do with the rules and laws and politics of the north! This is the beginning of a war that caused many to lose lives and the resolution that once the north had won all states were united as one! They swear never to fight a Civil War like that ever again. How different things may have been if the south would have won? Well, after slaves were emancipated and began to build communities of their own, many race riots had broken out after the Klu Klux Klan was formed to teach pesky smart Negroes a lesson of discipline because most southern bias white men continued to have a bitter taste in their hearts after their defeat in the Civil War, so they figured since we were considered to be inhumane, they inflicted their vengeance out on the Negroes. After all, the northerners had to return back up north, while most Negroes were too afraid to leave the place they had known as home. This decision resulted in the many lynching and loss of life and the raping of the Negro women. I wouldn't be surprised if some black men was raped as well in the same way the movie *Pulp Fiction* depicted! The most heinous crimes against Africans are just stories untold. Facts are the racist white men had nothing more to do but become creative. After all, if you date further back during the Pilgrim era, their methods were very creative and brutal, building all sorts of machinery of torture; thus, the idle mind has always been focused on torture and maiming enemies or anyone that opposed their power of authority. Of course, that only explains why so many slaves were too afraid to rebel. After all, the slaves were the cooks. They could have simply poisoned the entire household of their slave master, but they were very afraid because of all sorts of cruel unusual examples and psychologically well-thought-out agendas to break and domesticate a human being into the modest loyal "house Negroes." I can understand the black slaves' lack of options. They had to comply, but in today's time, I don't understand how these house Negroes can permit themselves to become involved in black-on-black crimes while saying they are Christians. I thought Jesus died for the sins of man, but Christians today will engage in black-on-black crimes before they lose their position of employment. Jesus gave his life for man. Was it the right thing to do? After all, some so-called Christians will not risk breaking a fingernail, let alone assist any other black man that endures a system designed to prevent superior advancement. Blockades are created to hinder such progress. So is it true that the Bible quotes that everybody that thinks they are going to heaven will not get there? The truth is the hearts of all humankind is measured in the likeness of God. That only describes that one must have the grace within and the wisdom to know that the wicked is mostly always considered the oppressed people who act out because of being tired of tyranny. And if you are one to work with a system design to deceitfully discriminate, are you not compared with the hang-man of the gallows? That thing that is ruled with evil intent enforced by Godly people with the knowledge of knowing and not attempting to become the Harriet Tubman of our time, attempting to remove the obstacles that you are able to remove after all if you don't help each other how do you expect any outside assistance. Thus, if it is evil intent, then the creator of its design is not of God. So how can you call yourself a worker of God, when God is not your employer with such evil intent and design? Who is your true master of deceit? Many topics related to racism and the crimes committed, people allow themselves to become evasive vague thinkers of a non existent facts permitting one self to phantom the thought which is always spoken by people who pretend or just refuse to acknowledge the truth they usually stipulate these exact words "get over it already!" My response to that is! I was never under it! Understanding that God have blessed me to see most of all things for its true nature. Only a person's guilt shall convict his conscience. Anyone who reads this information becomes enraged with truths and facts that racism is alive and well. Maybe for some unknown reason bias sits well with this individual. That means that racism is a form of hate and human emotion. Thus, it is being evolved from humans, which only defines that many humans are responsible for enforcing so many laws and regulations that are double standard and only affecting certain races of people, that which has been engraved into the black slaves genetically because of many years of torture and cruel and unusual treatment, creating the makeup of how we act, the things we do, and the hate of one another. Racism and slavery are one of the reasons why gangs exist and the reason why drugs flood our ghettos. They are the reasons why our city is called ghetto. Is there such a word for a white ghetto? These are the reasons why the Black Panther movement was decimated to prevent the advancement of strong, outspoken, unified black men with purpose and intellect. The assassination of Martin L. King, Malcolm X, John F. Kennedy, Robert F. Kennedy, and many more unsung heroes who have died addressing the discrepancies that are behind the scenes because of the hate of race and color of skin. The jealousy is deep within some men. Many hate crimes occurred nearly 150 years ago when slaves were set free. Actual race riots have existed as far as mankind can think back. Off the records, I would assume because murder has been around since Cain and Abel. Even in modern times, these sorts of riots exist, but why is the heat so intense between blacks and whites? Even though blacks are at the bottom, why does it seem as if it's either black or white, and everything else is just in between? Most riots that have occurred within the last 120 years have involved whites and blacks being among the stats of the most murdered fallen victims of warfare, or shall I say rioting blacks severely suffered the forefronts of brute force? Most of their murders were inflicted upon whites to combat the vicious assaults in self-defense! Modern-day riots normally ignite after some sort of police shooting or use of excessive force. Many blacks have reached their boiling points because of the emergence of hate crimes exercised by white bigots. Yet black-on-black crime, I suppose, it's formidable and acceptable with most Afro-Americans. Until something happens big, racially, then we all forget about the indifferences and status quo of rival gangs, burying the hatchet; and we unite for a common goal as a people!

As I depict "the good, the bad, and the ugly," so many young black men and women have endured a life of crimes and lies, suffering drastically because of the forced hand they were dealt with because of an unfortunate upbringing, a dysfunctional home that was poverty stricken, surrounded by family members who were deeply involved with a vital sickness called crack. This disease affected and plagued a race like monopoly flooding certain particular areas of America. To be specific, black and Latino communities were hit hardest by this epidemic. Drug addicts and drug-inflicted children grow up in a household without the presence of a father figure, always upset and angered at the world void of leadership and positive influences, such as role models. Kids who were without positive influences tend to gravitate toward the street life, where the gangs are effectively active and always more than willing to accept our youth with open arms. Gangs are always recruiting. It will always be the machine in essence of war and violence that changes with time and the young is how it survives. And it maintains to become larger than life, forever growing in a society that is built on bloodshed, lies, murder, and deceit. The gangs are just the mere image of its creator, and the children who succumb to its jaws of death are just imitating the people who we call leaders, our poor politically righteous teachers of a society with so many rules and laws enforced, which produces one to become corrupt and rebellious. How our tainted leaders rule and lead by example, and once we follow in their footsteps, we are considered criminals. The double standards that we abide by seems to only set us up for failure. Two steps forward are more like five steps backward. Every element seems to be set in play, adding fuel to this intense inferno. There are so many angles of loop holes of prevention of advancement from court hearings, lack of employment, lack of assistance, lack of education, lack of financial help, lack of moral support, eviction procedures, legal fines that take away from your very minimum employment wages or source of income, and bills that overcharge you with hidden fees. All these rules and laws to govern mankind and increase your advancement in progress seem to only depress you more and with stress constantly adding to the struggle as the rich gets richer and the poor pays all the taxes hiked up in poverty zones. This lack of development that the poor people endure mostly in Afro-American communities affects families to the point of breaking disaster. It turns a good mother into a drug-addicted individual, searching for a way to find liberation and an escape from all her worries. Boys grow up too fast and die young, forced into the deadly jaws of the streets. Innocent little girls lose their virtues, becoming displaced and demoralized to become a possession of exploitation as a sex toy. While the family suffers, the children suffer more, watching from the sidelines as their parents' demeanor and spirits are being ripped to shreds before their own eyes. The innocence of the children who endure watching their parents' life degenerate without any choice in the world. These are sometimes the children who end up taking chances with the streets and gangs only in the essence of becoming a product of this unfortunate environment as an attempt to seek to help his/her struggling parents or siblings who suffer the lack of supplement and nourishment that food provides. Thus, here lies the recipe why so many youth are actively involved in gangs as they witness and endure the pain of their parents' struggles, and it seems as if everyone is sentimental in this dog-eat-dog world, not a helping hand or a pillow to cry on anywhere. All this anger builds up inside, reaching an alarming explosive peak of detonation to that point that living seems to be a curse and death seem more rewarding. So it is that much easier to act out in the form of a menace, because anger, hate, and resentment are the things that have created the boys of our ghettos into killing machines—lack of all these above reasons! It is easier to seek revenge. In your mind, you don't care about dying, and your mentality is fuck the world because no one ever helped me or my family! Once blood is tasted, it is bittersweet! A monster in the making is created. Our own Frankenstein is born, and we are the doctors that have created this unruly killing machine. Because we lack all the above, because everything I mentioned explain how black people sitting at desk are killing more people than they would like to confess. They don't pull the triggers, but they surely contribute to the outcome of a monster, a menace in the making. Ask yourself the reason because I've already said it. You now have to figure out how is it so, because so many niggers act like house niggers, unwilling to assist each other. But we are so fast and ready to slam doors on other blacks who need moral support or legal assistance! How can our children become unified after they experience so much hate and resentment from people of color? The scales tip over, and the menace in our society is thus created, molded from so much he or she has endured and witnessed. They grow up feeling hopeless and lost, and a desire increases to engage in crime activities. How can you, with an honest face, say crime doesn't pay after it helps feed a poor hungry family? This creates exposure to the life of crime! A child that has no food resorts to crime as a source of supplement. Now he is exposed. If he gets caught, he has two strikes against him: his color and now a criminal record that will follow him like a dog leash and prevent further elevation in the future. Thus, when the times get harder, his chain is constantly snatched, with the burdens and discrepancies of rules, laws, double standards, poverty, and a family that is displaced. He begins to feel hopeless. He resorts back to the life of crime, which has somehow kept him fed and has protected him in other scenarios! Teach a child how to fish, and he will learn how to fish for a lifetime! So if doing wrong to do what is right, all that is reasonable to him without any concern during his parents' trials, how can you prevent this kid from going down the path that eats men alive? Each man that has been eaten alive once was this kid! Some of us were fortunate and have not lived or endured such disadvantages, growing up with a silver plate and spoon and everything that could be desired. They wouldn't understand why. They only think that those who didn't make it were lazy or didn't try hard enough. Some of us are unlucky. The difference between an officer and a criminal is one got caught and the other did not! After all, corruption starts from the top or does it start from the bottom working its way upward? I dismiss the statements that all men are equal because so many double standards exist in this world, and as a youth, you notice how standards are set up to cause failure! When I am told one thing, I endure the opposite. Many words of broken promises, but not much execution of effort! Thus, the gangs become that much more alluring and enticing. After all, we are one and the same who have all lived in the belly of the beast, so if society doesn't care, the street gangs always have an extended arm. This is why the gangs have more recruits than the American army! Because number one, we are all a product branded from our environment.

Growing up in this concrete jungle, running, ducking, avoiding gunshots, dodging the stray bullets that fly by mysteriously, whistling through the air, roaring, crackling ferociously, loud, biting, rippling through flesh like a kinsu blade or a sheet of paper being shredded! Corpse after corpse, life after life, victims lie in the streets, bleeding to death as their souls gravitate toward the heavens. Undirected, these missiles seek out to destroy, shattering windows into thousands of pieces after weapons are discharged. Guns are fired day after day, month after month. Days seem like years! When these gang wars go on seeming to last for eternity, bullets ricochet, bouncing off concrete walls, striking innocent bystanders.

Growing up in this intense battlefield, an innocent kid void of corruption desires excitement, and all he wants is to go outside and shoot marbles and fly kites. While the gangs engage in warfare, shooting humans and their victims, souls take flight to a different dimension. Kids play in their sandboxes, discovering bullet-riddled corpses! Now is that sanity for an innocent child? As he witnessed so much chaos, he becomes traumatized. He begins to have restless nights, waking up drenched with sweat covering his entire body, compelled by nightmares constantly invading his pleasant dreams. This is not normal as kids live in a place so dreadful, without any way out, forced to endure death daily! With so much death, our young children's hearts become barren and blank, unable to allow any tears to form and fall down their tormented cheeks! We are responsible. If anyone has a child and you live this vicious lifestyle, you are held accountable for teaching your sons and daughters how to die rather than live! Someone has to stop the domino effect. Starting with yourself, lead by example! Kids are afraid of their environment, afraid of their life! Enduring the things they have seen daily, encountering some unthinkable or unspeakable event, when you witness too much! Everyone knows the golden rules of survival. Hear no evil, speak no evil, see no evil. Remember saying too much in this concrete jungle could get you missing in this concrete jungle! No place and no one is excluded. The children's sandboxes are tainted and spilled with the blood of the innocent. The ruthlessness of the hoodlums was without mercy, and they never seemed to show any regard for human life! These monsters are careless and show no remorse! Their hearts are cold and blank, empty like the darkness in the midst of the night. Not realizing that even as they play god, God has the true power over their life, and their antics are useless. And punishment is just a step away. Live by the gun. Die by your deeds! They say you are what you eat! How can you resist not becoming like that which you endure? It is symbolic. Every day in your environment, you protect yourself while living as the fluffy white rabbit trapped and cornered in a lion's den, with ravaging carnivores drooling from their mouths like savages, with blood in their eyes and hatred within their hearts. This predatory instinct flows through their veins, with evil intent in their hearts! They want to eat you alive! The ghetto has always been like an jungle, and its inhabitants are much more like the beast of the jungle. An animalistic cave manlike monstrosity comes to life, diverting away from the human like qualities. Their misconduct and behavior consume even its own babies like cannibals!

With so much being mentioned, I can go on for many days discussing issues about racism and gangs. These are such dense topics that no one likes to talk openly about. I was once told by a wise man that to know what the problem is, you have to trace back where it began. That is why I have ventured as far back as slavery to find out why gangs and drugs coexist in the ghettos and why there is so much hatred between race groups and the all-but-familiar black-on-black crimes. Experience is my teacher because I am a product of my environment. I have been to prison, and many times thereafter, I have continued to find myself in trouble of my actions and sometimes a victim of the design. I was poverty struck and was affected by a fatherless household and drug-addicted family members who I loved. I watched as my mother's demeanor and dreams of aspirations were torn to shreds because of a drug called crack. I've been in displaced in foster homes. I begin a life of crime because my family lacked financial progress. I stole and burglarized commercial buildings to help feed myself and my family of eight who I lived with, overcrowding a one-bedroom apartment. I attempted to sell crack at the age of fourteen, even though I hated drug dealers after I watched my mother's life fall apart after my father's death. After all the pain she endured, I was forced to watch eviction after eviction. All that I suffered led me into the streets and into the arms of my new family, the gang. I learned to watch and become like every street legend before me. The streets became my school, my education, and my future because I felt hopeless and lost. I begin to fantasize about death and dying young, like most youth of today's era. Violence became essential to survival. I felt as if I had been stepped on and dragged through the mud. Most of my existence at that point, my actions of unruly behavior, defined my attitude, reflected as a kid with a death wish because of an unjustified childhood filled with so much pain and burdens. I always had a way with words, a God-given gift. Despite my affiliation, I continued to remain in school, and I loved to write. Many times I was informed to attend college to advance my skills, but of course, I only finished eleventh grade. After so many attempts on my life and so many trials, growing up, I finally figured things out. At age twenty-five, I decided to make a big move and change for the best. My life and experiences have paved the way and illuminated all the things that a young black youth endured. I know because I'm living proof. I hope that some kid reads this and decides to change his/her life before it gets too late because some way, somehow, we all have hidden talents. We just have to find out who we are first and blossom from that point thereafter. I am a product of my environment, and if I can gradually change, then anyone can change and become larger than life. First and foremost, God is the one who have made everything possible. Like rappers of the world, I will give all my thanks to him for moving mountains and walking with me when I was blinded by the lifestyle that has no true good outcome.

Follow your dreams, never give up, and don't let anyone ruin your dreams and aspirations. Peace and prosperity be with you.